LOGOS AND LANGUAGE IN THE PHILOSOPHY OF PLOTINUS

John H. Heiser

Studies in the History of Philosophy
Volume 15

The Edwin Mellen Press
Lewiston/Queenston/Lampeter

B
693
.Z7
H39
1991

Library of Congress Cataloging-in-Publication Data

Heiser, John H.
  Logos and language in the philosophy of Plotinus / John H. Heiser.
    p. cm. -- (Studies in the history of philosophy ; v. 15)
    Includes bibliographical references.
    ISBN 0-88946-288-7
    1. Plotinus--Contributions in philosophy of languages.
  2. Plotinus--Contributions in philosophical methodology. 3. Logos.
  4. Languages--Philosophy. 5. Methodology. I. Title. II. Series:
  Studies in the history of philosophy (Lewiston, N.Y.) ; v. 15.
  B693.Z7H39   1990
  186'.4--dc20   89-27514
                                                  CIP

This is volume 15 in the continuing series
Studies in the History of Philosophy
Volume 15 ISBN 0-88946-288-7
SHP Series ISBN 0-88946-300-X

A CIP catalog record for this book
is available from the British Library.

The Edwin Mellen Press   The Edwin Mellen Press
Box 450   Box 67
Lewiston, New York   Queenston, Ontario
USA 14092   CANADA L0S 1L0

The Edwin Mellen Press, Ltd.
Lampeter, Dyfed, Wales
UNITED KINGDOM SA48 7DY

Printed in the United States of America

LOGOS AND LANGUAGE IN THE PHILOSOPHY OF PLOTINUS

TABLE OF CONTENTS

INTRODUCTION

It is only recently that scholars have begun to take serious notice of the role language plays in Plotinus' philosophy.[1] This is not surprising. Plotinus did not, like Proclus, compose a commentary on the *Cratylus*. He rarely refers to the *Cratylus*, and then only to avail himself of one of Plato's fanciful etymologies, not to address Plato's problem. His other references to language are not made for their own sake, but to illustrate some other philosophical point. You might argue that a philosopher who claims there is "no *logos*" of his First Principle has said something significant about language. Perhaps he has, but it is, after all, something negative, and even here Plotinus does not proceed, as he might have done, to support this claim by analyzing or even explicating what it means to "say."

Still, studies have begun to appear which bear on one or the other aspect of "saying" in Plotinus.[2] I would like, in this study, to see whether

---

[1] As late as 1982, Jean Pepin, in "Linguistique et théologie dans la tradition platonicienne," *Langages* n. 65 (1982): 91-116, was remarking with satisfaction on the ever-growing interest historians have been taking in ancient philosophies of language (p. 91). But he still felt constrained to say that "contrary to what one might think," Plotinus too assigned a considerable role to language in his philosophy (p 94).

[2] For example, in addition to Pepin's article itself, Annick Charles-Saget, in *L'architecture du divin: mathématique et philosophie chez Plotin et Proclus* (Paris: "Les Belles Lettres," 1982) pays considerable attention to "la parole," especially in the chapter "Silence et *dianoia*" (pp. 95-103), and in the conclusion (pp. 299-309). See also Frederic M. Schroeder, "Saying and Having in Plotinus," *Dionysius*, IX (1985): 75-84; and the article by A. C. Lloyd, "Non-discursive

something more comprehensive might not be possible. I am less disposed than some to find incoherence in Plotinus' thought, even in his *obiter dicta*, and I am convinced that his remarks on language and *logos* embody a coherent and thought-out philosophical theory.

Those familiar with Plotinus will not expect from him anything resembling a contemporary theory of language. He is not at all interested in what a "competent speaker of the language" can or cannot do, or about the role language plays in common life. He is interested only in its role in philosophy itself, understood as the search for and ultimate attainment of the First Principle. Consequently, no study of his views on language can be comprehensive in any even minimal sense unless it ranges over his metaphysics as a whole. This would be true of any subject that finds a place in Plotinus' philosophy, but it is especially true of his views on language because of language's role as the instrument of philosophy. Any study of Plotinus' philosophy of language which treats language as an isolated phenomenon is bound to be wrong in principle and likely also in detail.[3] So I shall spend a preponderant amount of time on what may seem tangential issues. I can only say that I know of no other way to determine exactly what Plotinus means on a subject which is itself tangential to his main interests. You cannot do this by simply collating the few texts that bear directly on the issue.

Thought – an Enigma of Greek Philosophy," in the *Proceedings of the Aristotelian Society* , New Series LXX (1969-70): 261-274, and the response by Richard Sorabji, "Myths about Non-propositional Thought," in *Language and Logos: Studies in Ancient Philosophy Presented to G. E. L. Owen* (New York: Cambridge University Press, 1982), pp. 205-314. Lloyd responds to Sorabji in an article in *Phronesis*, "Non-propositional Thought in Plotinus," Vol. XXXI (1986): 258-265.

[3] Sorabji's article (above n. 2) illustrates this. He has no difficulty refuting Lloyd's thesis by citing the plain words of Plotinus. But because this was his limited purpose, Sorabji leaves one with the impression that Intellect knows "propositions," or knows by forming, or entertaining propositions. As we shall see, Plotinus rejects this suggestion out of hand. Not surprisingly, Lloyd has no difficulty refuting Sorabji, also from the text.

Plotinus' *obiter dicta* on language must obviously be organized around their central and controlling concept. There are two candidates for that position: "naming" and "saying." The fact that Plato wrote the *Cratylus* has tended to focus attention on the first of these concepts in the study of his philosophy, but it seems to me that a complete account even of Plato's views on language ought to treat naming within the larger context of "saying." Even in the *Cratylus* Plato's remarks on naming only make complete sense when we bear in mind that, for him, to name means – or ought to mean – to "say what something *is*" – to indicate its *ousia*. The *Theaetetus* and *Sophist* may tell us more about language than does the *Cratylus*.

With Plotinus there can be no hesitation. What interests him about language is the fact that it "says," and primarily that it says something to the very sayer. So this study will not be so much a study of language as a mere means of communication, as it will be of language as the embodiment of thought – of *logos*. The Greek word *legein* is even more closely related to what words *convey* than is the English word "say." "How are you saying that?" is not a question about phrasing. It means "what do you mean by that?" Hence Aristotle's famous expression: "things said in many ways" – terms with multiple meanings. To "say nothing" means, not to remain silent, but to speak nonsense or not to the point; and to "say something" means to have a point. Thus a Greek philosopher's views on "saying" lead one quickly beyond language to metaphysics, and a study of Plotinus' views will achieve that integration with his philosophy as a whole without which those views make little sense.

So the reader must not imagine that I am offering a new interpretation of that philosophy as a whole in the light of Plotinus' views on language. Even if it were possible, which it plainly is not, I have no desire to transform Plotinus into a primitive analytic philosopher, either to render him more palatable to current tastes or to save something from the supposed wreckage of his metaphysic. Anyway, who is to say his metaphysic is that total a wreck?

Neither do I intend to spend time conjecturing how Plotinus might answer the questions that preoccupy twentieth-century philosophers of language. Many, if not most, of those questions are based on assumptions Plotinus does not make. Among these is the very assumption that one's theory of language is, or ought to be, an area distinct from one's metaphysic. As readers of Plotinus know, not even his epistemology or psychology form areas distinct from his metaphysic. I believe Plotinus has something to say to us which is worth hearing, but we will not hear him unless we are willing for the moment to suspend belief in our assumptions and let Plotinus answer the questions he himself asks. If this in turn inspires us to reexamine our own assumptions, so much the better for philosophy.

CHAPTER I
"GIVING A *LOGOS*"

Commentators have long recognized the importance of language in Plotinus' *way of doing* philosophy. Both the written and the spoken word have an altogether central role to play. He was notoriously not interested in being original, and was certain that the writings of the ancients – Plato particularly – were a fountain of wisdom, even if they were sometimes "enigmatic."[1] We should look for more in an ancient's words than first appears, so it is not surprising that Plotinus gives the ancient sayings both exegesis and dialectical examination.[2]

Plotinus' own writings reflect a philosophy developed through the spoken word. With their frequent dialectic of question and answer, they embody an oral teaching which Porphyry describes as done through "lectures" (diatribai),[3] but lectures frequently interrupted by questions and occasionally supplemented by papers and counter-papers read by members of his circle.

---

[1] On this see especially Alain Eon, "La notion plotinienne d'exégèse," *Revue Internationale de Philosophie*, XXIV (1970): 252-289; see also A. Hilary Armstrong, "Tradition, Reason and Experience in the Thought of Plotinus," in *Plotino e il Neoplatonismo in Oriente e in Occidente* (Rome: Accademia nazionale dei Lincei, 1974), pp. 171 194.

[2] See Emile Bréhier, *La philosophie de Plotin* (Paris: Vrin, 1961), c. II, pp. 9-22.

[3] *Life of Plotinus* 3, 35. On the meaning and style of a "diatribe," see Bréhier's Introduction to his edition of the *Enneads*, 3rd ed. (Paris: "Les Belles Lettres," 1960), pp. xxvi-xxxvi.

The result may not be a Socratic dialogue, but it reveals an emphasis on oral interchange which was regarded as unusual in his day.[4]

Whether speaking or writing, Plotinus clearly regarded himself as engaged in what Plato calls "giving a *logos*." One of his favorite expressions is "*phesin*, or *legei ho logos*" (the *logos* says). In addition to "saying," the *logos* frequently "shows" (*phainei, deiknusi*), but sometimes it also "inquires" (*zetei*), and even "feels unsatisfied" (*pothei*). It is almost as if the *logos* had a life of its own, and in a certain sense it of course does.

What purpose does "giving an account" serve, in Plotinus' view? His answer to this question leads us into the heart of his philosophy of language.

Plato and "Giving a Logos"

We know Plotinus' thought, of course, from what we read in his treatises. We will not succeed in interpreting that thought unless we pay some attention to the background against which those treatises were written – the common fund of questions, concepts and presuppositions Plotinus shared with his readers. This background is the product of what has come to be called "Middle Platonism," an interpretation of Plato's writings with considerable borrowing, more or less conscious, from Aristotle and the Stoics. Porphyry tells us the treatises were written on questions which arose during Plotinus' philosophical conferences (*Life* 4, 10-12; 5, 61-63), and that these conferences usually began with readings from treatises and commentaries by Middle Platonists or even by Peripatetics (*Life* 14, 10-17). There is no evidence, from what Porphyry tells us, that they ever read Plato

---

[4] *Life of Plotinus* 3, 36-38; 13, 8-18. The treatises Plotinus wrote as a result of his oral teaching and discussions were not meant to be read by just anybody, but only by trained philosophers. Plotinus seems to have shared Plato's distrust of the written word as a means of instructing beginners. See John Rist, *Plotinus: The Road to Reality* (New York: Cambridge University Press, 1967), p. 9.

himself, or Aristotle. Still, commentaries presuppose the original texts, and Plotinus himself occasionally refers to the originals.[5]

Much of the literature of Middle Platonism has since disappeared, and any reconstruction is at best conjectural. In any case there is no way of knowing what Plotinus and his friends were reading at any given point. But we can sketch at least some of the background of the treatises by examining what the originals had to say. What was there to read, not what they "really meant." The latter question has no bearing at all on how Middle Platonism, let alone Plotinus, used them. But we can reasonably assume that Middle Platonism's "questions, concepts and presuppositions" stem ultimately from these originals.

With Socrates, Platonic philosophy in embryo was a matter of the spoken word–discussion, or, more precisely, "asking and answering questions."[6] As such, it could not be anything but a cooperative enterprise. In the *Protagoras* Plato characterizes this as "giving and receiving a *logos*."[7] One who knows, as the *Phaedo* says, proves it by being able to "give a *logos*" of what he knows.[8]

As late as the *Phaedo*, the "method of *logoi*" described there remains a cooperative venture. Socrates' reasoning has to satisfy others who might object, and the "satisfactory hypothesis" one finally reaches seems to be one satisfying all parties (101D). But in principle the procedure Socrates

---

[5] Father Paul Henry, in "Une comparaison chez Aristote, Alexandre et Plotin," *Les sources de Plotin* (Geneva: Fondation Hardt, 1960), pp. 429-449, even finds one instance where, he believes, Plotinus was comparing the words of a commentator, in this case Alexander of Aphrodisias, with those of the original, in this case Aristotle.

[6] See *Gorgias* 449B; *Cratylus* 390C and 398D; *cf. Gorgias* 457C-458B; *Protagoras* 329A and 336C.

[7] 336C; *cf.* 338D; *Republic* I, 344D.

[8] 76B; *cf. Symposium* 202A; *Republic* VII, 534B.

describes could be carried out in the privacy of one's own mind, even though not so expediently or surely. And in any case the one giving an account is in that very act coming to see the truth for himself – or rather to "recall" it – within his own soul.

In the *Republic*, one able to "render an account to himself and to another" of the *ousia* of each thing is identified as the master of "dialectic." But with the *Republic*, versions of the dialectical process begin to appear which discussion with others might initiate and promote, but which reach their completion in a synoptic vision that could hardly be found outside the soul itself by itself.[9]

The *Republic* still identifies this "dialectic," at least in its early, learning stages, with the old Socratic question and answer (see 538D-539A). Aristotle's *Topics* are evidence that a Socratic form of dialectic continued to be practiced in the Academy and probably also in the Aristotle's own Lyceum.[10] But with Aristotle this Socratic dialectic is an exercise distinct from philosophical thinking proper (*Topics* VIII, 1, 155b7-12). Its value lies in its preparing the ground for philosophic insight into first principles (*ibid*. I, 1, 101a34-b4).[11] Plato's own later thinking on philosophic method seems to have been headed in that same direction as he gradually departed from the Socratic model. Plato's use of aporetic (and hence Socratic) dialectic as a "training exercise" in the *Parmenides* (see 135C-136C) suggests as much.

---

[9] VI, 511B-C; *cf*. VII, 532A-B; 533C-D; and espec. 540A-B; *cf*. also *Sophist* 253B-D; *Phaedrus* 265D-266B; *Philebus* 16B ff.

[10] See Gilbert Ryle, "Dialectic in the Academy," in *New Essays on Plato and Aristotle*, ed. Renford Bambrough (New York: Humanities Press, 1967), pp. 39-68, and another article with the same title in, *Aristotle on Dialectic: the Topics* ed. G. E. L. Owen (Oxford: Clarendon, 1968), pp. 69-79; Paul Moraux, "La joute dialectique d'après le huitième livre des *Topiques*," *ibid*., pp. 277-311.

[11] Bear in mind that, for Aristotle, a definition such as those Socrates was seeking is a first principle; see *Meta* VII, 9, 1034a30-32; *Post. An.* I, 2, 72a6-24; II, 3, 90b24-27.

When Aristotle explains the preparatory role of aporetic dialectic ("going through the difficulties") in *Metaphysics* III, 1, he might almost be commenting on the latter half of the *Parmenides*. But Plato did not, like Aristotle, reserve the name "dialectic" just for Socratic exercises like this. He also gives it to his new method of dividing and combining Forms (*Sophist* 253C-E; 259E). As for Plotinus, he seems never to have looked for, and hence never to have found any development in Plato's thought. Instead he tried to find a description of "dialectic" that would cover all the roles Plato assigns to it anywhere in the dialogues. We will examine this description later.

Still, even philosophical thinking, however defined, remains thinking (*dianoia*), a process Plato describes in a famous passage of the *Sophist*:

> ...thinking and discourse are the same thing, except that what we call thinking is, precisely, the inward dialogue carried on by the mind with itself without spoken sound...whereas the stream which flows from the mind through the lips with sound is called discourse.[12]

What Aristotle thought of this description of thinking we have no way of knowing, but on two occasions Plotinus seems to be alluding to it.[13] Undoubtedly he would accept it as in some sense true, but as we shall see he has a more nuanced theory of what goes on in the mind than this. To the degree one accepts this way of viewing it, thinking remains bound up with language.

---

[12] 263E (Cornford); *cf. Theaetetus* 189E-190A.

[13] VI. 9 [9], 10, 6-7: "...the science involved with demonstrations and proofs and the dialogue (dialogismos) of the soul"; V. 3 [49], 3, 3-4: "...unless, perhaps, the soul converses (dialogizoito) with itself and asks...." Aristotle could hardly have failed to notice that one can talk to oneself in the privacy of one's own imagination. He alludes to this in both *Topics* VIII, 14, 163b3-4 and *Meta* IV, 4, 1006b9. Whether this constitutes "thinking" he does not say.

6

Knowledge is another matter. One might suppose that, if thinking is the soul's inner dialogue, or, as the *Theaetetus* puts it, "asking itself questions and answering, saying yes or no" (190A), then the final judgment (*doxa*) that brings this process to an end is an inner statement. The *Theaetetus* accepts this conclusion (*ibid.*). It might also seem that when one reached this term one at least sometimes would have knowledge. But when it comes to *defining* knowledge, then a *doxa* that happens to be true, even when accompanied by a *logos* in some sense or other of that term, fails in the *Theaetetus* as a definition of what it means to know. Socrates eliminates each sense of *logos* by showing that one could have a true judgment and be able to give a *logos* in that sense and still not have knowledge. So, though there is never any doubt that he who knows must be able to give a *logos* of what he knows (see 202D), knowledge itself either involves *logos* in some new sense, or involves something in addition to *logos*. As will appear, Plotinus has his own views on how knowledge in the soul differs from the *logos* one gives of it.

Plotinus and "Uttering" a Logos

In his treatise "On Nature, Contemplation and the One" (III, 8 [30]), Plotinus explains the purpose served by "giving a *logos*." He distinguishes between the "learner" (*manthanon*, 6, 21) and the "accomplished sage" (*spoudaios*, 6, 36).[14] The *spoudaios*, he tells us:

> ...has already finished reasoning (lelogistai ede) when he declares what he has in himself to another, but in relation to himself he is vision.[15]

---

[14] The term *spoudaios*, especially in the Hellenistic age, came to characterize someone of achieved philosophic wisdom. It means "good" with overtones of "outstanding," "worthy," "impressive," "weighty," etc. Aristotle in his *Nicomachean Ethics* (I. 7, 1098a9-12) uses it to describe the accomplished lyre-player (as opposed to the mere dabbler), who serves as an analogue of the man of virtue.

[15] 6, 36-38. Extended passages from *Enneads* I-V are taken from A. H. Armstrong's translation in the Loeb Classical Library Series. Translators are expected to *translate*, no matter what. I have taken the liberty of putting some key terms, such as *logos*, *ousia* and

Plotinus does not tell us why the *spoudaios* speaks out, but presumably he is doing what Plotinus was doing when he lectured or wrote a treatise. Whatever that was, it was not a process of producing knowledge in the soul of the learner – even in the qualified sense in which Aristotle sees this happening.[16] For a *logos* to "teach" is for it to "remind the soul" (V. 1 [10], 1, 23-29), and what the soul remembers is "itself and what it possesses" (I. 6 [1], 2, 10-11). Although Plotinus uses the word *anamnesis*, or "recollection," in these contexts, he is somewhat uncomfortable with it because it suggests recovering something from the past, whereas the soul is really actualizing what is eternally present within it,[17] or rather, as we shall see, actualizing its true self.

Whether or not the learner is being guided by a teacher, the *logos* that issues in recollection is one that comes from within the learner. Plotinus agrees with Plato that the learner learns, not by *hearing* a *logos*, but by *giving* one. But this is not, or at least not necessarily, by the dialectical interchange of question and answer. The learner "utters" his *logos* all right, but for his own inspection, not for the inspection of a Socratic midwife:

> The soul...when it has become akin to and disposed according to the *logos*, still, all the same, utters and propounds it – for it did not possess it primarily – and learns it thoroughly and by its proposition becomes other than it, considering it, like one thing looking at another. ...it does not go on uttering what it

---

noesis back into a transliterated form of the Greek when they occur. Passages from *Ennead* VI are my own rendering, as is the occasional detached phrase from elsewhere.

[16] *Post An* I, 1. This passage acknowledges the active side of the learning process, but the teacher is still a *cause* of knowledge in Aristotle's view. See *De Gen et Corr* II. 11, 335b21-23; *Phys* VIII. 5, 257a1-3, 12-13; *cf. Soph Elench* 2, 165b1-3; 10, 171a37-b2.

[17] IV. 3 [27], 25, 27-35; *cf.* IV. 7 [2], 12, 8-12; I. 2 [19], 4, 22-25; III. 7 [45], 1, 20-25; V. 3 [49], 2, 11-14. Only when he is arguing *ad hominem* with the Gnostics does he allow *anamnesis* to look to the past. See II. 9 [33], 12, 4-8.

has uttered well already, but what it utters, it utters because of its deficiency, with a view to examining it, trying to learn thoroughly what it possesses.[18]

This "utterance" could be taking place in the privacy of the learner's mind, but it appears to be a verbalizing utterance nonetheless. Cilento is right, I think, to see in this passage allusion to the Stoic *logos prophorikos* (uttered *logos*) and *logos endiathetos* (*logos* situated within), not only in the recurrence of the word "utter" (propherein), but also in the term here translated "disposed" (diatethe).[19] Plotinus allows for the possibility of an inner utterance (although he does not call it that) – the reception into the imagination (phantastikon) of the *logos* which manifests thought (IV, 3 [27], 30, 6-11). When this happens, we become conscious of the thought which is always present within us, whether we are conscious of it or not.[20] This may well be Plotinus' equivalent of Plato's "soul conversing with itself."

---

[18] III. 8, 6, 20-33; *cf. ibid.*, 3, 13-15; *cf.* also V. 8 [31], 11, 1-16: "...one of us, being unable to see himself, when he is possessed by that god [Intellect] brings (propherei) his contemplation to the point of vision, and presents (propherei) himself to his own mind and looks at a beautiful image of himself; but then he dismisses the image...and comes to unity with himself, and, making no more separation, is one and all together with that god silently present...to begin with he sees himself, while he is different from the god; then he hastens inward...and is one with that higher world....While he is coming to know the god he must keep to an impression of him and form distinct ideas of him as he seeks him and discern what he is entering into...." V. 8 is a continuation of the treatise on contemplation (III. 8). As the comment on this passage in the Harder translation points out, verbal echoes of the former passage appear here. See *Plotins Schriften*, Übersetzt von Richard Harder: Neubearbeitung mit griechischen Lesetext und Anmerkungen, fortgeführt von Rudolf Beutler und Willy Theiler, III b (Hamburg: Felix Meiner, 1964), pp. 395-396. The most significant of these echoes is "propherei," which is the word for "utter."

[19] *Paideia antignostica: Riconstruzione d'un unico scritto da* Enneadi *III, 8; V, 8; V, 5; II, 9* (Firenze: Felice de Monnier, 1971), pp. 138-139. The term "propherein" reappears in VI. 6 [34], 9, 17-21, where Plotinus compares "uttering" what is within oneself to the creative act by which Soul produces the sensible universe. As we shall see, this is not just poetry.

[20] More goes on in the soul than just reasoning, of course. There is the entire appetitive life of man. So Plotinus attributes to "perception" (aisthesis) generally the function of becoming aware of one's inner life. But this inner speech seems to be our way of becoming conscious of reasoning. On the relation of consciousness to imagination, see also IV. 8 [6], 8; V. 1 [10], 12; I. 4 [46], 10; and *cf.* I. 1 [53], 11, 5-9. Also H. R. Schwyzer, "'Bewusst' und 'unbewusst' bei Plotin," in *Les Sources de Plotin*, pp. 341-390.

By "giving a *logos*" to himself, then, the learner recovers awareness of the intelligible world present within him. This process, which Plotinus calls "thinking" (dianoia), or "reasoning" (logismos), is the characteristic activity of the embodied soul as such.[21] This is the activity the *spoudaios* is finished with, except for "declaring what is within him to another." This means, as we shall see, that the *spoudaios*, "in relation to himself," is no longer functioning as an embodied soul.

For Plotinus a "part" of the soul is always present in the intelligible, and hence must be eternally in the act of thinking, whether we know it or not (see, in addition to the above passages, IV. 8, 4, 29-32; III. 4 [15], 3, 21-28; IV. 1 [21], 1, 12-17; VI. 4 [22], 14, 16-31; IV. 3 [27], 8, 11-18; 12, 1-6). Startling as this may appear, it is surely the most coherent way to make sense of the Platonic *anamnesis*. At any rate, it is Plotinus' way, although he knows how startling it is (IV. 8, 8, 1-4).

[21] Henry J. Blumenthal, in *Plotinus' Psychology* (The Hague: Martinus Nijhoff, 1971), argues convincingly that the *dianoetikon* and the *logistikon* are one identical power of the soul (pp. 100-111). But when Plotinus is referring to the act of philosophical reasoning, he tends to use *logismos* rather than *dianoia*. The latter is a more general term for any kind of discursive thinking.

CHAPTER II
THE ASCENT TO INTELLECT

On more than one occasion, Plotinus remarks on the affinity our reason has with the sensible world. Even when speaking of the eternal intelligibles, we seem compelled to use temporal[1] and spatial[2] expressions. This affinity of reason for the sensible makes it difficult for us to conceive how the intelligible world is present to the spatial world of sense. Plotinus devotes one of his longer treatises – VI. 4-5 [22-23] – to persuading the reader that the intelligible world, mediated by Soul, is present whole and entire everywhere. He complains:

> The reason (logos) which attempts to submit what we have said to examination is itself not something one, but rather divided, and in its enquiry it makes use of the nature of bodies and takes its principles from there. It supposes *ousia* to be that sort of thing, and divides it up, and does not believe in its unity, all because it did not start its enquiry from the proper principles.[3]

---

[1] V. 1 [10], 6, 19-28; V. 8 [31], 12, 26-27; VI. 7 [38], 35, 27-29; III. 7 [45], 6, 22-27; 11, 11-14.

[2] V. 1 [10], 10, 7ff.; V. 2 [11], 2, 19-23; VI. 8 [39], 11, 13-28.

[3] VI. 5 [23], 2, 1-6. See also V. 9 [5], 5, 9-11; IV. 3 [27], 20-23, espec. 20, 42-51, and *cf*. III. 6 [26], 12, 28ff. and V. 5 [32], 9. Plotinus' use of images and metaphors to illustrate the intelligible, a practice that will become such a prominent feature of later neo-Platonism, would seem to be a concession to this weakness of reason. V. 8 [31], 9 is an excellent example of an image at work. This aspect of Plotinus' style has received considerable attention since R.

Logos *and the Forms*

If our *logos* is so sense-bound, how can it lead our souls out of the Platonic cave and into the intelligible world? Plotinus has a psycho-ontological explanation of this which we will examine later. But there is a more fundamental logico-ontological explanation which he tends to accept as already established by Plato – the doctrine of Forms and their participation.[4] In Plato's allegory of the cave there is one element of cave-life which transcends the shadows – names, and hence language. In applying names to the shadows on the wall, the prisoners are misapplying to these copies names which really belong to their originals.[5]

In the *Cratylus* Plato had investigated the act of naming. There he had argued that names are meant to distinguish the being (ousia) of things (388B-C), and therefore ought to be coined by "dialecticians" (390C). Unfortunately the "legislators" who have been doing this adhere to the philosophy of flux, so that they coin names inappropriate to genuine *ousia* (439B-440D).

Ferwerda's *La signification des images et des métaphores dans la pensée de Plotin* (Groningen: Wolters, 1965) and Peter Crome's *Symbol und Unzulänglichkeit der Sprache* (München: Wilhelm Funk, 1970).

[4] There is a sort of proof for the existence of Forms in V. 9 [5], 3. At any rate, Plotinus appears to be identifying it as a proof when he refers to it in II. 4 [12], 4, 1-2. A similar line of argument appears in V. 8 [31], 5. But in general, Plotinus appears to be no more interested in proving that there are Forms of sensible things than Plato is, but for different reasons. He is much more interested in what I call the "psycho-ontological" approach to the intelligible world – soul turning inward and thereby discovering its own nature and the nature of its source.

[5] *Republic* VII, 515B; *cf. Phaedo* 78E and *Timaeus* 52A. There is a textual problem with the *Republic* passage, but as Maurice Nedoncelle points out in "Les données auditives et le problème du langage dans l'allégorie de la caverne," *Revue des sciences religieuses* XLIV (1970), 168, the various editors who cannot agree on how to emend the text are in perfect agreement on the meaning it intends to convey. Nedoncelle's article as a whole is very much worth reading.

Plotinus identifies these mythical legislators with Soul.[6] This is not a
bad choice, if one insists on turning every Platonic myth into an allegory. It is
surely Plato's point that names are a creation of reason; only, disappointingly,
it is a reason living on the level of sense, opinion and flux.

This may write off *the way names are formed* as being of little help
toward discovering the natures of things, but the *act of naming itself*
(predication) still purports to be determining the being of the thing
named – to be saying something of *what it is* – however ineptly the name may
have been formed by the legislators. According to the *Republic*, budding
philosophers are led to question the propriety of this act of naming when
they notice that opposite names are applicable to the same sensible object, so
that such objects "are and are not" what they are said to be.[7] This turns the
intellect away from such things and towards its true object – what simply "is,"
rather than "is and is not." Thus the philosopher comes to realize what things
really deserve the names he had previously been misapplying to their
shadows.

Plotinus accepts this account of things, although he usually follows
Plato's *Timaeus* by settling on the most obvious form of being and not-
being – becoming. It is their mutability that excludes sensible things from the
realm of true being.[8] Nevertheless, "what truly is," i.e., the Forms, and "what
becomes," i.e., sensible particulars, are called by the same name. Why?

When present-day commentators ask this question, they frequently
mean: what makes Plato (and Plotinus) think that forms are "self-
predicating" – that squareness is square, and horseness is a horse? It is

---

[6] V. 5 [32], 5, 23-28. *Cf. Cratylus* 401C.

[7] VII. 523B-524D; *cf.* V. 479A-C; *Phaedo* 74B-E; *Parmenides* 128E-129E.

[8] IV. 7 [2], 8₅, 48-50; V. 9 [5], 5, 35-37; VI. 5 [23], 2, 9-16; III. 6 [26], 6, 76-78; VI. 2 [43], 1, 20-
21. *Cf. Timaeus* 28A3-4.

14

sometimes suggested that they were led into this "logical blunder" by the peculiarities of Greek idiom, which refers to squareness as "the square itself" and horseness as "the horse itself." To this last Plato could surely counter: how do we know we are not being misled by *our* idiom into missing his point? As to self-predication, people, including Plato, were of course "predicating" long before Aristotle coined the term. But Plotinus' thought, like Plato's, focussed on an aspect of this act which we may overlook if we treat it as a mere logical operation. It is the act by which the mind purports to lay hold of "what truly is," with its necessary self-identity. To ask if forms are self-predicating takes for granted just what Plato finds problematical. It sees no problem in predicating "square" of square objects, and just wonders whether it can also be said of squareness. Plato's problem is not whether squareness is square or horseness is a horse, but rather, how in the world you can call anything square which, the next time you look at it, is oblong. How can you call anything a horse when the next time you encounter it, it is dog food? Names ought to designate being – *ousia*. What is constantly changing ought not be called being, but becoming.

Since, in Plotinus' view, "the intelligibles are not outside the intellect," as *Ennead* V. 5 [32] puts it,[9] we might be tempted to think that the horse destined for the cannery is a horse, and the Form of horseness is the (divine, creative) thought of a horse. Thus they would be identical in the way the thought of a thing is identical with the thing thought about. This might even seem to be the meaning of the following passage:

> When things have being together with matter (meta hyles),
> their being is not in the intellect. But [the *genera* being,

---

[9] This expression appears in the title, and titles were given to the treatises by Plotinus' disciples, not by the master (*Life* 4, 17-19). But there is no reason to suppose Plotinus was unaware of these titles, and this one expresses succinctly just how he reads Plato.

movement and rest] are non-material. When things are non-material, if they are understood, this constitutes their being.[10]

Despite the Aristotelian echoes of words like these, Plotinus will have nothing to do with such an interpretation. Since the Form is the cause of the (prospective) sensible thing, it must obviously be prior to that thing. But if it is, in its very nature, nothing but the thought of the thing it will cause, the thing will be prior to the form. In the nature of things, the object of thought is prior to and defines the thought of it. Consequently "the square itself" and "the horse itself" cannot be mere thoughts. They must be something in their own right – be an *ousia*. Only in this way can they be objects of Intellect's thought.[11]

So how do Form and particular receive the same name? Plainly because the particular is an image of the Form and thus participates somehow in its reality. What I see in the mirror every morning is me in a certain sense – it certainly is not anybody else. But in a more profound sense it is not me – not in the way I am me.

Plato wrestles with this question of names in *Timaeus* 49B-50C. Later (52A), in summing up his conclusions, he uses the term "homonymos." In his day the term simply meant "having the same name," but with Aristotle's *Categories* (I, 1 a1-3), it came to mean "having the same name but a different *logos* (definition) corresponding to the name." In *Ennead* III. 6 [26], 7 ff., Plotinus is attempting to employ Aristotle's term "matter" (hyle) in a way consistent with what Plato says in the *Timaeus* about the "receptacle." In Plotinus' account, the images in "matter" are called "falsehood" (*pseudos*, 7,

[10] VI. 2 [43], 8, 3-5; *cf.* V. 9 [5], 5, 12-23.

[11] The passages that affirm this priority of being over thought are V. 9 [5], 5, 17-23 and 7, 9-18 and VI. 6 [34], 6, 5-30; but I do not believe these passages are completely clear without the light VI. 7 [38], 8, 1-13 throws on them. It is worth pointing out that even for St. Thomas Aquinas the Divine Ideas are not just "divine thoughts." The *Divine Essence Itself*, understood as imitable in various ways, is the idea of various creatures (*ST* I, 15, 2c).

37-44), matter is called a "liar" (*pseudetai*, line 22), and the images that appear in it come "falsely into falsehood" (13, 33-34). They have the same name as their Form, but "homonymously," apparently in something like the Aristotelian sense.[12]

Despite all this insistence on the "falsehood" of the image as opposed to the "true" original, we are obviously not dealing with sheer equivocation – what Aristotle calls "chance homonymy" (*Nic Eth* I, 6, 1096b26-27). Aristotle's sensible *ousia* may be, in Plotinus' eyes, a "so-called *ousia*,"[13] but Plotinus is not disposed to call the horse in its stall a "so-called horse." It shares a common name with the intelligible horse because, in a way, it *is* that intelligible horse on a lower level.

Judging by the way Plotinus talks about "we" in I. 2 [19], 3, 19-33 and I. 4 [46], 3, 17-24, the Platonic tradition must have hit upon its own version of "things said in many ways." It appears to have applied the term "homonymous" to the naming of originals and their images, by including them among "things said by priority and posteriority," or "primarily and secondarily." Of course in Aristotle's "homonymy by relation to one" the name was said in a prior and primary way of the "one" and in a secondary way of the rest, but this Platonic version of homonymy could hardly be regarded as just a special case of Aristotle's focal homonymy. In the passages mentioned above, Plotinus is referring to Intellect and Soul, its derivative, as "things said primarily and secondarily." But what he says in the context of both passages implies that he thinks of Forms and sensible particulars in the same way.[14] The Form "horse" and the horse in the pasture are called horse "homonymously" by priority and posteriority.

---

[12] 17, 21-26; *cf.* VI. 2 [43], 7, 8-14; VI. 3 [44], 1, 6-7; 20-21; 16, 5-7; 22, 16-18.

[13] VI. 3, 2, 1-4; 5, 1-3; 9, 1-2; 15, 25-26.

[14] I. 2 appears to reject the term "homonymous" in this context, but I. 4 adopts it without reservations. Platonists seem also to have put to rest the objections in Plato's *Parmenides* to

Creative Logos *and Uttered* Logos

At this point we have come upon one of the most supple and elusive doctrines in Plotinus – the doctrine of *logos* in its fully ontological sense. The doctrine owes something to Stoicism, and in one of his earliest treatises Plotinus criticizes the Stoic understanding of it:

> But if they are going to say that *logoi* are enough [to explain this universe], these must clearly be eternal; but if they are eternal and not subject to affections, they must be in Intellect, and in an intellect of this kind, one which is prior to condition and nature and soul (V. 9 [5], 5, 23-26).

Plotinus is thus willing to accept that there are "logoi" in sensible things, provided one understands that these *logoi* derive from and are more truly found on the level of Intellect. In fact, Plotinus comes habitually to use the term *logos* to designate the mirroring forth on a lower level of what is found more truly at a higher level of things – in Soul and ultimately in Intellect and the intelligible world. And since *logos* is a mirroring forth of Intellect, each level of *logos* is a higher or lower level of "contemplation."[15]

When one is attempting, as I am, to reconstruct Plotinus' philosophy of language, this concept tantalizes. The various senses of that protean Greek term *logos* are themselves not instances of mere chance homonymy. In his treatise on "Nature and Contemplation" (III. 8 [30]), Plotinus clearly means us to see an analogy between the "utterance" of the learner – his

---

the "resemblance" analogy. Plotinus needs only to remind his readers that the relation of image to original is not reciprocal (see I. 2, 1, 28-55; 2, 1-11).

[15] See the discussion of this subject that appears on pages 97-100 of *Les Sources de Plotin*, and cf. John M. Rist's chapter on "Logos" in *Plotinus: the Road to Reality* pp. 84-102, and John Deck's *Nature, Contemplation and the One* (Toronto: University of Toronto Press, 1967), pp. 56-63.

18

"giving a *logos*" – and the way Nature produces by conveying *logos* from Intellect to this universe.[16]

"Nature," for Plotinus, is the lower reaches of Soul – Soul as forming and informing the visible universe. Its analogy with the learner is complex and at first confusing. Plotinus begins by comparing the learner unfavorably to Nature. Nature, being *logos*, is a form of contemplation, as is the soul of the learner. But unlike the learner, Nature does not have to reason in order to discover what is within it (it does not "give a *logos*") (3, 13-14). Instead, it remains in silent and unmoved contemplation and simply makes (4, 1-13). In this it is more like the *spoudaios*. Does this mean that, on this account, Nature is higher in the scale of being than the soul of the learner? Not at all. Plotinus goes on to discuss "soul that is prior to nature" (5, 2), and by this he does not mean just the World Soul, which also and *a fortiori* produces Nature from its contemplation without reasoning.[17] He means soul with its "love of learning and spirit of enquiry, its birthpangs from the knowledge it attains and its fulness" (3-5); *that* soul, not just the World Soul, is prior to nature because it attains a clearer vision (8-10). In fact, in the company of World Soul, it *produces* Nature as a contemplation dimmer than itself (6). All souls are, after all, essentially the same – are in fact one soul, though of course not one to the exclusion of all multiplicity.[18]

This being so, one has to take the analogy between Nature's creativity and the disciples' utterance rather more seriously than one might otherwise have done. The analogy serves to integrate Plotinus' version of *anamnesis*

---

[16] See especially chapter 6 and *cf.* VI. 6 [34], 9, 17-21.

[17] IV. 4 [28], 10-11; V. 8 [31], 7; VI. 7 [38], 1-3.

[18] See IV. 9 [8]; and *cf.* IV. 2 [4], 2, 52-55; IV. 8 [6], 2, 19-26; 3, 10-13; V. 1 [10], 2, 1-10; IV. 3 [27], 1, 18-22; 2, 1-5; 33-49.

with his metaphysics of participation and thus introduces the "psycho-
ontological" account of language I referred to above.

Plotinus does not represent Soul, *via* Nature, as "uttering" the
Universe like some cosmic *logos prophorikos*. He uses the Stoic term "utter"
exclusively for human verbal utterance. But *logos*, whether it is being
"uttered" by a learner or simply emerging on a lower level of reality as
Nature's creation, is always an "unfolding" (anaptyssein)[19] or an "unrolling"
(exelittein, anelittein)[20] into multiplicity of something more truly
itself—because more one—at the higher level of Intellect. It is always an
expression and explication of a higher and more unified contemplation. As
regards utterance, he puts the matter succinctly in two passages which will be
the central and thematic texts for the remainder of this study:

> ...just as *logos* in its utterance is an image of *logos* in the soul, so
> soul itself is the *logos* of Intellect (V. 1 [10], 3, 8-9; *cf.* 6, 45-46).

> As the spoken *logos* is an imitation of that in the soul, so
> the *logos* in the soul is an imitation of that in something else.
> As the uttered *logos*, then, is broken up into parts as compared
> with that in the soul, so is that in the soul as compared with
> that before it, which it interprets (I. 2 [19], 3, 28-31).

Both these passages concern soul in its relation to Intellect, and
Plotinus does not here elaborate on how, precisely, the uttered *logos* is the
"broken up image" of the *logos* in the soul. It is by no means obvious how an
utterance is the "image" or "imitation" of the thought it signifies. Plato's

---

[19] Plotinus uses this term exclusively for the process of mental explication: IV. 3 [27], 30, 9;
IV. 4 [28], 1, 25; VI. 7 [38], 1, 40; 2, 18.

[20] *Exelittein* is used both of creative explication: IV. 8 [6], 6, 8; V. 7 [18], 3, 15; IV. 3 [27], 5,
10; III. 7 [45], 11, 24, and of mental explication: V. 8 [31], 6, 10. It is also used for the
"unrolling" of Forms within Intellect, a matter we will be considering later: III. 8 [30], 8, 34-36;
VI. 7 [38], 9, 38; VI. 8 [39], 18, 18-20; V. 3 [49], 10, 52.
Analittein's one use is mental: I. 1 [53], 8, 8.

Cratylus says often enough that *names* "imitate," or ideally ought to imitate, the *ousia* of the things they name (422E ff.; 430B ff.; 439A ff.). This they would most likely do by having root sounds which suggest basic characteristics of things (424A ff.). It is notoriously difficult to determine how seriously Plato meant his attempts to apply this principle – his etymologies. I suspect he meant the principle seriously but had little faith in specific applications. In any case the "legislators" will have bungled their job through faulty philosophy, so that they cannot have achieved the mirroring forth of *logos* Plotinus describes here.

Plotinus himself has no comment to make on Plato's project in the *Cratylus*, and his occasional use of a Platonic etymology is not enough to indicate his view of the matter. It would be a mistake to see the present remarks on "uttered *logos*" as such a comment. We do not, after all, recognize what words mean by etymological conjecture.

The "image" analogy in general is no doubt based on the *Republic's* "shadows and reflections on water or other smooth surfaces" (VI, 510A). These "look like" what they imitate as well as deriving from it, but no Platonist, least of all Plotinus, was so crude as to suppose that visible resemblance is part of the notion of "imitate" – it is resemblance in "what a thing is," not in "how it looks." In like manner, auditory resemblance need not be an essential element of vocal imaging, whatever the role mimicry may have played in word creation. There is an obvious identity between what we say and what we think which would seem to be all that is necessary. In fact, Plotinus' words make it plain that this ability of words to "embody," "convey," "express" thought makes them the primary analogue of the *logos* relationship in general, and thus the source of meaning for the other analogues.

That is why I see these two texts as "central and thematic" for a study of *logos* and language in Plotinus. They tell us what language says and how it says it. Plotinus adapts the Stoic term *logos* to a Platonic metaphysics by including overtones of "expressing," even a quasi-"uttering." *Logos* is not just a rational principle found in the sensible world. It is the mirroring forth of Intellect. In the same way, what language "says"–says primarily–is not the sensible things that confront the sayer. Plato may be right, and the "legislators" may have tailored the names in our language to fit this world of fleeting images. But since sensible things *are* images, their names, like their reality, are not properly their own. Their names are borrowed names for a borrowed reality. By "giving a *logos*" to itself, the philosophic soul can discover the true reality within itself. This true reality is what language really utters, or ought to utter–something within the knowing soul–the very Intellect which gives *logos* to the world.

Logos *and Opinion*

This unfolding of *logos* into multiplicity plainly does not proceed directly from Intellect *via* Soul into speech unless one's *logos* derives from genuine knowledge (episteme). There are, after all, mistaken opinions, partially correct opinions, and opinions that chance to be correct but remain, for all of that, mere opinions. Such opinions are obviously not simple images of what is in Intellect. Still, they cannot be entirely divorced from Intellect either. The soul is, after all, "in Intellect," and it is hardly likely that it would be completely unaffected by that presence. What everyone says with assurance–a *koine ennoia*–even if they cannot give a *logos* of it, is likely to embody the truth.[21] A philosophical theory which renders meaningless names everyone uses is, to say the least, suspect.[22] The "ancients" especially are likely to have hit on the truth, some more clearly than others, some phrasing it better than others, even though they may not spell out their

---

[21] VI. 5 [23], 1, 1-8; *cf.* VI. 7 [38], 29, 10-19; III. 7 [45], 1, 1-9.

[22] VI. 8 [39], 7, 11-24; see also III. 1 [3], 7, 13-16 and *cf.* V. 3 [49], 13, 23.

logos.[23] Even some of Plato's etymologies, at least when dealing with such fundamental notions as "being" and "one," indicate soul's presence in Intellect (V. 5 [32], 5, 23-28). But in all these cases you are still on the level of opinion until you have submitted such opinion to dialectical examination and given a *logos*. Still, *logos* must somehow be in these opinions if dialectical examination can bring it to light.

One of Plotinus' two references to Plato's "inner dialogue of the soul" is a brief account of the way our everyday thinking deals with sensibly given objects. This account illustrates how Intellect illumines even this sort of thinking, at least when evaluations are involved:

> ...sense-perception sees a human being and gives its impression to discursive reason (dianoia). What does reason say? It will not say anything yet, but only knows, and stops at that; unless perhaps it asks itself "Who is this?" if it has met the person before, and says, using memory to help it, that it is Socrates. And if it makes the details of his form explicit, it is taking to pieces what the image-making power gave it; and if it says whether he is good, its remark originates in what it knows through sense-perception, but what it says about this it has already from itself, since it has a norm of the good in itself...because it is like the good, and is strengthened for the perception of this kind of thing by Intellect illuminating it (V. 3 [49], 3, 1-9; *cf*. ch 2).

Logos *and Science*

In addition to our ordinary thinking, there are "sciences in the rational soul." Even some of these do not simply mirror forth Intellect. These are the "so-called sciences" of sensible things "if one ought to speak of 'sciences' of these: 'opinion' is really the suitable name for them." These are "posterior to

---

[23] III. 7 [45], 1, 9-17; 13, 13-18; *cf*. IV. 8 [6], 1 and V. 1 [10], 8 and 9.

their objects and likenesses of them" (V. 9 [5], 7, 1-4).[24] Purely intelligible principles are at work in these sciences. The study of nature receives help from dialectic "as the other skills use arithmetic to help them, though natural philosophy stands closer to dialectic in its borrowing" (I. 3 [20], 6, 3-5). But to the extent that the study of nature remains dependent on the senses and is "posterior to its objects," it cannot represent the simple unfolding of intellect within the soul. This role is reserved for dialectic itself. Plotinus describes dialectic in his treatise on that subject. In so doing he presents his most comprehensive account of what it means to "give a *logos*":

> It is the science which can speak about everything in a reasoned and orderly way, and say what it is and how it differs from other things and what it has in common with them; in what class each thing is and where it stands in that class, and if it really is what it is, and how many really existing things there are, and again how many non-existing things, different from real beings. It discusses good and not good, and the things that are classed under good and its opposite, and what is the eternal and what not eternal, with certain knowledge about everything and not mere opinion. It stops wandering about the world of sense and settles down in the world of intellect, and there it occupies itself, casting off falsehood and feeding the soul in what Plato calls "the plain of truth," using his method of division to distinguish the Forms, and to determine the essential nature of each thing, and to find the primary kinds, and weaving together by the intellect all that issues from these primary kinds, till it has traversed the whole intelligible world; then it resolves again the structure of that world into its parts, and comes back to its starting point; and then keeping quiet

---

[24] The term *doxa* need not mean "mere opinion." Even "Plato's" views on the categories are referred to as *doxa* in VI. 2 [43], 1, 5 and VI. 3 [44], 1, 2. But when Plotinus refers to his own "doxai" these usually concern either this world or the soul's presence in it. See, e.g., IV. 8 [6], 8, 1; II. 1 [40], 1, 33; 2, 1 and 4, 10; III. 7 [45], 7, 15. In this he is being faithful to Plato, despite his propensity to allegorize the myths Plato uses in such circumstances.

(for it is quiet in so far as it is present There) it busies itself no more, but contemplates, having arrived at unity (4, 2-18).

When this process is completed, however many years it takes, one is presumably no longer a learner but a *spoudaios*, "all vision." The soul, having derived its principles from Intellect, "combines and interweaves and distinguishes their consequences, till it arrives at perfect intelligence (nous)" (5, 3-4). At this point one has passed beyond the activity characteristic of embodied soul – *dianoia* or *logismos* – and has reached the *noesis*, commonly described by commentators as "intuitive knowledge," characteristic of *Nous*, or Intellect.

CHAPTER III
INTELLECT

Plotinus' way of distinguishing Soul from *Noesis* and *Nous*, and relating Soul to them, bristles with difficulties.[1] Many of these difficulties no doubt stem from a radical ambiguity inherent in any Platonic account of the soul – an ambiguity that confronts Plato himself in *Timaeus* 34B-C. Virtually everything distinctive of the soul, as opposed to pure intellect, is due to soul's relation to body, yet you cannot allow that the soul is what it is because of its relation to body. That would make the soul, to use Plato's words, "younger than body." In addition to this, Plotinus' Soul, being an image and *logos* of Intellect, could really be called Intellect at a lower – because more multiple – level (see III. 8 [30], 6, 24-26). Distinctness must not be stressed at the expense of continuity.

Thus Intellect exists not only in itself, but also in soul as a "state" (hexis) derived from Intellect.[2] The soul can thus be said to have an act of intellection (noein) in a secondary and derivative sense (I. 2 [19], 3, 24-36). Plotinus calls the intellect in us the "dividing intellect" (merizon nous) (V. 9

---

[1] See Henry J. Blumenthal, "*Nous* and Soul in Plotinus: Some Problems of Demarcation," in *Plotino e il Neoplatonismo*, pp. 203-219.

[2] I. 1 [53], 8; *cf*. V. 9 [5], 3, 21-24, 33-37; V. 3 [49], 2, 14-23.

26

[5], 8, 20-23; see 9, 1-2), and tells us that our intellect "is in *logismois*" (V. 1 [10], 3, 14). And because not only "intellect in us," but also Intellect itself is present to us, "...we possess the Forms in two ways, in our soul, in a manner of speaking unfolded and separated, in Intellect all together" (I. 1 [53], 8, 7-8).

This means that the "intellect in us," functioning on the soul level, manifests itself in reasoning. Consequently, after years of exercise in dialectic, when one finally ceases to reason and attains the state of "quiet," "unity" and "vision" described in the treatise on dialectic, one has transcended the level of soul. One is thinking on the level of Intellect, and is, in fact, thinking through Intellect itself and as one with it.[3] This startling claim makes sense if we accept that continuity between soul and Intellect mentioned above. In Plotinus' hierarchy of *logos*, the lower *is* the higher at a debased level, and the higher is the "true self" of the lower.

Noesis

If the intuitive consciousness transcends *logismos*, you would expect *noesis* to be ineffable by definition. But there are two approaches reason can take so as to find something to say about *noesis* as a mode of knowing. Plotinus uses both of them. One approach begins with a consideration Plato seems to ignore, at least in his dialogues[4] – the relation between knower and known. Since this consideration is pivotal to Aristotle's account of intellect, we might call this approach "Aristotelian." The other approach we can call "Platonic," since it centers rather on the intelligible object itself, like Plato's own account.

---

[3] IV. 7 [2], 10, 30 ff.; IV. 4 [28], 2; III. 8 [30], 6, 14-19; VI. 7 [38], 35, 3-6; I. 4 [46], 4, 12-17; 9, 25-30; V. 3 [49], 3, 19-29; 4, 9-13 and 29-32; 6, 13-16.

[4] Unless he is touching on it in *Timaeus* 37A-C, as Aristotle believes (*De Anima* I. 2, 404b7-19).

Aristotle begins with the experience of our own intellect and the relation it has to its object. Knower and known are one only in the act of *noesis*. Taken in themselves, one is only a potential knower with no nature other than its receptivity; the other is form in matter, only potentially intelligible. He recognizes the defect inherent in that relationship, imperfect identity between knower and known, and eliminates that defect in his account of the pure act of intellect, which thus becomes intellect fully one with its object – thought thinking itself. Plotinus follows a similar line of thought, but very much *mutatis mutandis*.[5] "Intellect in us" is anything but a *tabula rasa*,[6] and its objects are by no means "forms in matter." Consequently the "otherness" to be overcome is not, as in Aristotle, that of a knower and a known that are, taken in themselves, only potential. Instead it is the otherness of the intelligible mirrored forth in the soul "as from another" and that same intelligible "in itself":

> Perhaps, then, we ought to teach our soul how intellect contemplates itself, and to teach that part of the soul which is in some way intellectual, since we call it discursively intelligent and by this naming indicate that it is a kind of intellect or that it has its power through and from Intellect. This therefore should know that in its own case too it comes to know what it sees and knows what it speaks (legei). And if it was what it speaks, then it would in this way know itself. But since the things which it speaks are above, or come to it from above, whence it also comes itself, it could happen to it, since it is a *logos* and receives things akin to it, and fits them to traces in itself, in this way to know itself. Let it then transpose the

---

[5] See III. 8 [30], cc. 6-8, espec. 8, 1-9; V. 3 [49], c. 6; and *cf.* V. 6 [24], c. 1 and VI. 6 [34], 6, 19-29.

[6] I happen to believe that what Plotinus says in IV. 4 [28], 2, 8-12 about a "self empty of all things" is directed against Aristotle's *tabula rasa*, but the correctness or not of this interpretation has no bearing on anything at issue.

image to the true Intellect, the one which (we observed) was the same as the truths it thought...(V. 3 [49], 6, 18-31; *cf.* 9, 1-28).

The soul, so long as it is functioning at soul level, "knows what it speaks," but "is not what it speaks." Intellect, on the other hand, *is* what it "speaks."[7] We will examine later what it means for Intellect to "speak." For the soul to "speak" is to express the Intellect that is in it by *logismos*. It must do this, according to III. 8, because it has not appropriated what is in it. Or as V. 3 has it, it must "fit" the image within it to the originals in Intellect.[8]

We can infer from this, in a somewhat Aristotelian vein, that separate Intellect must be one with what it knows, and that he who experiences *noesis* will be one with what he knows. But we can infer something more – that what Intellect knows, and what soul utters in order to come to know, is not the featureless unity, not the bare self Plotinus finds in Aristotle's separate Intellect.[9] It is the totality of the Platonic Intelligible World. This is certainly what we would expect if the soul's own elevation to *noesis* comes as the culmination of that process of dialectic described in I. 3.

So we have come upon the second, "Platonic" approach to *noesis*. This focuses not on the act of *noesis* and its relation to its object, but on that object itself – the being which the soul brings to unity by dialectic. Being is the "one-many" of Plato's *Parmenides* (144E),[10] and *noesis*, if it is the

---

[7] V. 3, 5, 25-26; *cf.* V. 5 [32], 2, 18-21.

[8] *Cf.* I. 2 [19], 4, 20-25: "Does the soul not recollect them? It had them, but not active, lying apart and unilluminated; if they are to be illuminated and it is to know that they are present in it, it must thrust towards that which gives it light. It did not have the realities themselves but impressions of them; so it must bring the impressions into accord with the true realities of which they are impressions."

[9] V. 1 [10], 9, 16-24; VI. 7 [38], 37, 1-5.

[10] V. 1 [10], 8, 24-27; *cf.* VI. 4 [22], 11, 15-20; VI. 6 [34], 13, 52-53; VI. 7 [38], 14, 11-12; VI. 2 [43], 15, 13-15; V. 3 [49], 15, 10-12.

knowledge of being, must be the comprehensive knowledge of the entire complex of Forms. It knows them as one by including their multiplicity in a single vision, not by transcending it. And it is vision of the "all," not some flash of partial insight. Plato's being is the "all" (*to on te kai to pan, Sophist* 249D), and even the "intellect in us" with which Aristotle begins is "intellect by becoming all things" (*De Anima* III. 5, 430a14; *cf.* 4, 429a18-19).

This is Plotinus' reasoned account of an intuitive knowledge he claims also to have experienced. Most of his remarks about *noesis* are consistent with the supposition that he is talking about a permanently acquired state of soul rather than a single conscious experience. The passages on consciousness cited in note 20 of Chapter One make it clear that consciousness of one's inner life is not necessarily an enhancement of that life; it may be a sign that we are functioning at less than our peak intensity. But some of what Plotinus says about *noesis* seems to mean that, on occasions, the *spoudaios* experiences a conscious union with the totality of being. I am not sure that a search elsewhere for comparable experiences throws much light on that.[11] As to the ordinary experience of the *spoudaios*, one who has mastered a subject and then casts about for ways to put it so that a beginner will come to "see" it may have an inkling of what Plotinus means by saying that the *spoudaios* is "vision."

The "One-Many"

In order to relate language to the intelligible thus understood, we must determine in what ways precisely the "one-many" is "broken up" at the level of soul, and how the "uttered *logos*" represents a further disintegration.

---

[11] Richard Wallis, "*NOUS* as Experience," in *The Significance of Neoplatonism*, ed. R. Baine Harris (Norfolk, Va.: International Society for Neoplatonic Studies, 1976), pp. 121-153, looks into the biographical literature for experiences comparable to Plotinus' claimed experience of intellection. He does not seem to have found any really close analogues of what Plotinus describes.

Plotinus says enough here and there in his writings that the answer to this is not just a matter of conjecture. To get the force of what he says, we ought to begin by describing the kind of unity present at the level of Intellect itself. Plotinus has not just intuited this mode of union. By negation of bodily conditions and by analogy with certain features of soul's *logismos*, he has worked out a *logos* of it.

If there is multiplicity within unity, you can reasonably speak of the many as "parts" of the one. But when it thinks of "parts," our reason, with its affinity for the bodily, tends to "divide up *ousia*." We must correct this propensity. It is characteristic of bodies as such that no one of their parts "is the same as either another part or the whole, and the part ...must necessarily be less than the whole." Perceptible masses "each have their own place" (IV. 2 [4], 1, 13-16). These conditions do not obtain in the incorporeal, where the many are many "by otherness and not by place" (VI. 4 [22], 4, 25; *cf.* 11, 15-18).

Plotinus insists that, with spatial conditions thus removed, the part is identical with the whole; that not only is the whole "infinite," but so is the part; that adding a part to the whole does not increase it, nor if, *per impossibile*, you could remove a part from the whole, would you diminish it.[12] The basis of this claim is not just denial of spatial conditions. Plotinus offers a positive reason for it. Unlike bodies, which are the aggregate sum of their parts, the intelligible is made up of "parts" which "derive from the whole" as a unity and "remain in that unity."[13]

This introduces the other element of Plotinus' account of the one-many. The whole is related to its parts as a genus is related to its species. Intellect as a whole contains all things "as a genus does its species and a

---

[12] VI. 4 [22], 5, 1-8; VI. 5 [23], 9, 12-18; 12, 1-7; III. 8 [30], 8, 42-49; V. 8 [31], 4, 22-25; 9, 19-23.

[13] VI. 4 [22], 4, 3-12; VI. 5 [23], 9, 31-40; V. 8 [31], 4, 22-25.

whole its parts" (V. 9 [5], 6, 10-11), so that "intellect as a whole is all the Forms and each individual Form is an individual intellect" (*ibid.* 8, 4-5).[14]

The genus-species relationship is essential to the process of *logismos*, and therefore appears on the soul level. If soul is a *logos* of intellect and the complex of Forms that dialectic "weaves together" is the content of intellect, then we should expect to find the genus-species relationship there as well, with suitable modifications. Sure enough there it is, as we discover in VI. 2 [43], with its analysis of the "Platonic" supreme genera: being, sameness, otherness, motion and rest.

Plotinus never calls Intellect itself a "genus"; it only contains the Forms "as a genus does its species." His reluctance to call Intellect a genus, at least in the context of his discussion of the "supreme genera," stems from the fact that "supreme genus" suggests not only supreme generality – Intellect certainly has that – but also membership in a *set* of genera, coordinated rather than subordinated to one another, so as together to generate the multiplicity of the intelligible world.[15] Intellect, on the other hand, is the entire intelligible world itself:

> The true Intellect is being together with all the rest [i.e., sameness, otherness, motion and rest]; as a result it is the totality of beings, whereas bare being by itself, taken as a genus, is an element of Intellect (VI. 2, 18, 13-15).[16]

---

[14] *Cf.* V. 1 [10], 4, 21-29; 9, 7-23; VI. 7 [38], 9 and 17, 25-39; VI. 2 [43], 20, 1-3; 21, 1-6. These passages make it clear that Plotinus continued to view the Forms as "particular intellects" long after he wrote V. 9, even though he never again put it that way explicitly.

[15] The other four supreme genera may "participate" in being, but they are not "species" of being. It is not predicated of them "as an expression of what they are" (en to ti esti) and so is not their genus (VI. 2 [43], 8, 41-47; *cf.* 9, 18-21; 15, 11-16).

[16] In II. 6 [17], 1, 1-6, he had tried out a similar distinction between being and *ousia*. By VI. 2 he has quietly dropped that idea, and now tends to treat "being" and "ousia" as virtual equivalents, in Plato's fashion. See 2, 44-46; 8, 12; 9, 13-15; 19, 19-20. *Cf.* Plato's *Sophist* 250B; 251D-252A; 258A-B.

These niceties aside, Intellect, regarded as containing its parts, is not only related to these parts in the way a genus is to its species, but Plotinus chooses it as a "sort of paradigm" of that relationship (19, 21-23). Plotinus constructs his account of the genus with great care, and seemingly in opposition to Aristotle's account. For Aristotle, not only is the universal not an *ousia*, since it cannot exist "separately" as an *ousia* must (*Meta* VII, 13-14; *cf.* 16, 1040b16-27), but the genus appears to be more removed from separate existence than the species. Of itself it is only "potential," or "matter," and requires the addition of a difference in order to be actualized in some *ousia*.[17]

For his part, Plotinus warns:

> We must be careful not to let the several genera disappear in their species, or the genus be nothing but a mere predicate, something contemplated in the species. It must be at the same time in them and in itself, mixed with them while remaining pure and unmixed; it must not contribute to the being of other things and in so doing destroy itself (VI. 2, 19, 12-17).[18]

Far from being a mere potentiality waiting for a difference to actualize it, the genus is the "principle" of its species (2, 10-26), in the sense that it "makes," or "generates" them (9, 9-10; 10, 32-42; 19, 1-2; 21, 1-12, 35-42).

Chapter 20 of VI. 2 contains Plotinus' own account of the way Intellect universal contains the particular intellects (the Forms) "as a genus its species." That account makes liberal use of the Aristotelian terms "potentiality" and "actuality" in a way Aristotle would never recognize. Plotinus' own treatise on "What is in Potentiality and What is in Actuality"

---

[17] *Ibid.*, VIII. 6, 1045a7-b8; *cf.* VII. 12, 1038a5-8 and 16, 1040b5-16.

[18] *Cf. ibid.*, 2, 19-27; 12, 10-14.

(II. 5 [25]) is hardly any more help toward understanding this extraordinary passage. That treatise rules out "being in potency" in the sense of "capacity to become" as having no place in the intelligible world (3, 1-32). This is no surprise, and it leaves the active "power to make" as the only appropriate sense of "potentiality" in the eternal world (24-26).[19]

This sense is indeed the key sense of "potentiality" in VI. 2, 20. According to this chapter, the universal Intellect is the "potentiality" of the particulars (lines 25-26), clearly in that active sense mentioned in II. 5. It "makes" them. The consequences of this are the key to the entire passage. As the productive power of the particulars, the universal Intellect is necessarily prior to them, contains them in its universality (lines 14-15) – they are "latent" in it (lines 26-27) – and it is "actually all of them taken together" (line 21). Nothing could be farther from Aristotle's "genus as matter." A Plotinian genus is *more* actual than its species rather than less. Plotinus calls it the *choregos* of its species (line 13), a term applied to the wealthy citizen who funds the dramatic chorus as his public duty. All this is certainly in keeping with the general principle that the one is prior to the many, the source of the many, and consequently more actual than the many. We must bear in mind that the relation of genus to species in Plotinus is not a mere "logical" one. A Plotinian genus is not a "concept" – a "mere predicate" as Plotinus says. It is a principle of *being*, and its relation to its species is an ontological one. Even the term "logico-ontological," which I have used in another context, would probably be misleading here. The relationship is rather the ontological foundation of what will emerge *on a lower level* as a logical relationship.

---

[19] A meaning not unknown to Aristotle. See *Meta* V. 12, 1019a15-23; IX. 1, 1046a9-29.

But having said all this, Plotinus goes on to say that the universal Intellect "is potentially" each particular taken separately (lines 21-22).[20] This introduces a new sense of "potentiality" for which II. 5 has done nothing to prepare us. He certainly does not mean that Intellect universal "is able to become" the particulars. Still, if it "makes" them *within itself*, so that they remain identical with it in some way, then it is hard to see how else one could phrase it except to say that it is they "potentially." If they are *it*, explicated, then it, explicated, is *they*. Considered, therefore, as prior to them and (eternally) "about to make" them, it "is they potentially."

How they are *it* "potentially" (lines 22-25) is the real puzzler; all the more so because Plotinus takes this to imply not only that they, as parts, are identical with the whole as whole, but that all the other parts are somehow "in" any given part,[21] so that it is identical with them as well.[22] One might suppose that a particular intellect, if it is in any way comparable to a species, would be a partial manifestation of the genus at best. It might then *participate* in its genus, but not, surely, be the whole of it, even "potentially," let alone be all the other species.

But this is still to misunderstand the Plotinian genus, which must be *as a whole* in each of its particulars (VI. 2, 12, 10-13). It is not a bodily mass to be cut up and parcelled out. Nor is it Aristotle's "genus as matter." It is "all the species taken together" and the "potentiality of them all taken separately"–*that* is what is in each particular "as a whole."

But how does that allow you to say that they "are it potentially"? In VI. 2, 20 Plotinus alludes to the way a particular science includes science.

---

[20] IV. 8 [6], 3, 14-16 speaks in a similar way: universal Intellect "potentially includes" its particulars, while they actualize its potentiality.

[21] VI.4 [22], 4, 42-43; III. 8 [30], 8, 43-44; V. 8 [31], 4, 7-9.

[22] VI. 5 [23], 7, 1-8; III. 8 [30], 8, 42-49; V. 8 [31], 9, 16-28.

Plato's *Sophist* (257C-D) may have suggested this to him, as well as the fact that the "sciences in the soul" are a *logos* and unfolding of Intellect. Plotinus had investigated the unity and multiplicity of science on a number of occasions before he wrote VI. 2, sometimes to illustrate the unity and multiplicity of Intellect, but more often that of soul.[23] On some of these occasions he spoke of "potentiality and actuality."

The theorems of a science "potentially contain" the whole of that science, seemingly because they *derive* from it and without that derivation would not be scientifically knowable. This suggests that the "potentiality" by which particular intellects "are potentially" Intellect universal is not a potentiality *in them* – certainly not one by which they "can become" Intellect universal. Instead it is that same active potentiality by which it is able to make them, and consequently contains them "potentially."

But however one construes the terms, it seems evident that what universal Intellect and particulars are "in actuality" is what each is "in itself." What they are "in potentiality" would then mean what they are as one with each other, "in" each other, "mixed."[24]

If we find this account of the genus less than convincing, we should remember another consideration that seems to have been at the back of Plotinus' mind. This is the special relation of identity he sees existing between Intellect, whether particular or universal, and the "all." He owes this to the Platonic transposition of Aristotle I mentioned above. Here is Plotinus' clearest statement of this relationship:

> ...Intellect is not the intellect of one individual, but is universal;
> and being universal, is the Intellect of all things. So, if it is

[23] V. 9 [5], 6, 4-8; 8, 5-7; 9, 2-4; IV. 9 [8], 5, 8ff.; III. 9 [13], 2, 1-4; VI. 4 [22], 4, 43-45; VI. 5 [23], 10, 47-50; IV. 3 [27], 2, 50-55; V. 8 [31], 4, 48-51.

[24] See the passages referred to in footnote 18 of this chapter, and the associated text.

universal and of all things, its part must possess everything and all things: otherwise it will have a part which is not intellect, and will be composed of non-intellects, and will be a heap casually put together waiting to become an intellect made up of all things.[25]

If we are still not convinced, Plotinus might blame this on the fact that genus and species on the level of *logismos*, where we ordinarily encounter them, have not this degree of unity. It is time to see in what way this unity is diminished at that level.

---

[25] III. 8 [30], 8, 41-46; *cf.* VI. 4 [22], 3, 31-35; VI. 5 [23], 7, 1-7.

CHAPTER IV
RATIONAL UTTERANCE

It is a plain fact of experience and a scandal to many philosophers that the soul is not fully aware of all that it has within it. If you are a Platonist, and subscribe to *anamnesis*, it is important that this be so, and be seen to be so. In his treatise on self-knowledge, V. 3 [49], Plotinus allows the reasoning power (logistikon) only a very limited and qualified knowledge of itself. It knows the "impressions" (typoi) it receives from the outer world through sensation and the "impressions" it has from Intellect within. It is aware that it is a reasoning power, and that it reasons by relating sense-impressions to memories or images retained in the imagination, or to the intelligibles it has from Intellect, or even by relating intelligibles one to another. From this last it can discover that it is derived from Intellect and is its image (cc. 2-4). It achieves full self-knowledge only through union with Intellect, and then, of course, it is knowing its "true" self rather than its derivative self (cc. 5-6).

The soul learns what it has within itself by being aware of its own reasoning acts, perceived by imagination as inner speech, as we saw above. From this evidence Plotinus infers that we have "intellect in us." He also adopts elements from Aristotle's psychology, finding in us acquired habits

38

(hexeis) of science,[1] art[2] and virtue.[3] He is, of course, no Aristotelian when it comes to explaining how we acquire such habits, or even what "acquire" means in such a context.[4]

We will be looking at the unity of science when we contrast it with the multiplicity of utterance. More basic to our rational life is the multiplicity of "intellect in us" in contrast with the unity of Intellect itself. Intellect in us, the "dividing intellect," manifests itself in reasoning. What is distinctive of reasoning is that it considers "one thing after another" (V. 1 [10], 4, 20-21), that is, it considers the intelligible world part by part rather than in synoptic vision.[5] In an earlier chapter of VI. 2, chapter 3, Plotinus had this to say about the unity of the "one-many":

---

[1] On *hexeis* in general, see I. 1 [53], 11, 7-8; on science as a *hexis*, see IV. 4 [28], 12, 7-9; VI. 2 [43], 18, 9; on dialectic as a *hexis*, see I. 3 [20], 4, 3.

[2] V. 9 [5], c. 11; IV. 4 [28], 11, 7-8; 12, 8-9.

[3] I. 3 [20], 6, 7; II. 5 [25], 2, 34-36.
[4] It means to "recover" by the Platonic "purification" and "separation" of soul from body (*Phaedo* 64C-67D). See Jean Trouillard, *La purification plotinienne* (Paris: Presses Universitaires, 1955). IV. 4 [28], 12, 7-14 seems to imply that habits are in some sense "acquired," but just before he wrote the treatises "On Difficulties about the Soul," of which this is one, Plotinus had been at pains to show, in III. 6 [26], chapters 1-5, that, in such "acquisitions," the soul itself remains "essentially unaltered" and does not "undergo" anything. Plotinus wants to take advantage of Aristotle's claim that the soul, as such, does not undergo change, without buying the rest of the package, that the soul is form of matter. Whether he succeeds or not is fortunately not relevant to this study.

[5] In his paper before the Aristotelian Society, A. C. Lloyd suggested that Plotinian intuitive knowledge would resemble "thinking, or thinking of, say, beauty, without thinking something about beauty, say that beauty is truth" (p. 261, *cf.* pp. 268ff.). Since he seemed to know that, for Plotinus, intuitive thinking "involves thinking of everything at once" (p. 267), it is difficult to say in what way it was supposed to resemble "thinking of, say, beauty." The mere fact that you can think of beauty *rather than* wisdom, even if only to predicate truth of it, shows that you are on the level of *logismos*. At this level it is not surprising you feel compelled to proceed to predication. This is not only consistent with, it is a necessary consequence of, Plotinus' view, as we shall see.
In his 1986 article, Lloyd corrects this. There he takes intuitive knowledge to be the knowledge of "generic being," (p. 263) and to "ignore" the division into species (p. 265). But to consider A and ignore B is still the function of *logismos*. Professor Lloyd appears to be treating the Plotinian genus as if it were a concept of some sort – though admittedly a strange one – and even an element in a Plotinian "logic." If there *were* a Plotinian logic, it obviously

Perhaps we should not call this unity the cause of the other beings at all, but say rather that they are, as it were, its parts or elements – that they are all one nature which is divided by our thoughts (epinoiais), and that due to its amazing power it is one extending to all, revealing itself as many and becoming many as if by a sort of movement. Thus the rich fecundity of its nature would be what made the one to be not-one; and we, by uttering its quasi-parts, would be making each of them a one and calling it a genus, failing to realize that we had not seen the whole of it at once. But as we utter it part by part, we put the parts back together again, since we cannot for very long hold them back as they strain towards themselves. And so we let them go to the whole and allow them to become one, or rather to be one (20-32).

Rejoining the parts seems to be Plotinus' way of describing predication – or "weaving the Forms together," to use Plato's phrase (*Sophist* 260A). We cannot rest with an isolated subject; we must reunite it with its predicate. Or rather, since we ourselves are responsible for its original isolation, we must "let it go back."

Distinction in Logos

The dividing function of "intellect in us" gives meaning to two expressions from the traditional philosophical lexicon. Plotinus makes use of both of them, one in the passage cited above. Either in "thought" (epinoia) or "formula" (logos) we can divide or separate what is one in Intellect. The expression "separate in *logos*" derives from Aristotle, and when first we encounter it in Plotinus he is criticizing an Aristotelian use of it. Aristotle

could not be located above the level of *logismos*. In fact, Plotinus locates logic even lower on the scale – at the level of utterance, as we shall see. Professor Lloyd is aware of this ("Neoplatonic Logic and Aristotelian Logic – I," *Phronesis* I [1956], p. 58) but he does not seem to have asked himself why Plotinus takes this view. And he still believes you can treat the genus as if it were merely a logical term in Plotinus (*ibid.*).

tells us that matter and privation are one in subject but twofold in *logos*,[6] but he does not supply us with these *logoi*. Since the only *logos* you can give of matter is the privation of all *logos*, matter and privation must be identical in every way (II. 4 [12], c. 14). But Aristotle's misapplication of the distinction in this context does not prevent Plotinus from using the expression himself in other contexts.[7]

Distinction in *epinoia*, the expression he uses in VI. 2, 3, has virtually the same meaning as distinction in *logos*, as his use of it there and elsewhere reveals. It too seems to be an expression from the traditional philosophical vocabulary. The way he uses it in criticizing the Gnostics suggests it is a phrase familiar to them as well as to his readers.[8]

As Plotinus' criticism of Aristotle indicates, a distinction in *logos* is not just a distinction of names, and one cannot simply "make" such distinctions at whim. The same is true of distinctions in *epinoia*. The Gnostics distinguish between "intellect knowing" and "intellect knowing that it knows," but this distinction cannot be made even in *epinoia* (II. 9 [32], 1, 52-54). This is not just an impossibility "for thought," as if it had no relevance for the thing known by that thought. If things can be separated in thought, this points to a multiplicity in things themselves – not a separation, but a multiplicity. Thus, VI. 2 argues that the two genera, being and movement, may be one (since true being is in act, and its act is the movement of life), but they are also two, since we can separate them in thought (here the term is *noesis*), which we

---

[6] *Phys.* I. 9, 192a2-33. Aristotle does not say this exactly; it would be strange to describe matter and privation as being "identical in subject," when matter is itself the subject in which privation inheres. Plotinus, or one of the peripatetic commentators he used, reads this into Aristotle, possibly influenced by the way Aristotle explains action and passion and their common subject, motion, in *Phys.* III, 3, 202b19-22.

[7] See II. 5 [25], 3, 15-18; IV. 3 [27], 9, 16-20; VI. 7 [38], 18, 31-36; 40, 15-18; VI. 8 [39], 1, 35.

[8] II. 9 [33], 1, 38-54; see Cilento, *Paideia Antignostica*, pp. 227-228. For other occurrences of the term, see V. 9 [5], 5, 9-11; VI. 6 [34], 6, 36-37; VI. 8 [39], 13, 1-4; VI. 2 [43], 7, 18-20.

could not do if they were not two (7, 6-24). Likewise when intellect knows itself, knower and known are not other except in *logos*; but this is enough to make it a plurality, so that what is absolutely one cannot have *noesis* even of itself.[9] We must not make the One twofold "even in *epinoia*" (VI. 8 [39], 13, 1-4).

On the other hand, "any composition (synthesis) can be broken down into its parts in *logos* and *dianoia*" (IV. 3 [27], 9, 19-20). And when the same attribute is predicated of two things that differ, we can consider that attribute separately in *logos*, as we do the genus that is predicated of its species or an attribute predicated by priority and posteriority (VI. 7 [38], 18, 31-36). So the "dividing intellect," by its separate considerations, is tracing out distinctions within the inseparable unity of Intellect itself.

To call the division our reason makes a "logical" or "conceptual" distinction is to evoke possible connotations foreign to Plotinus' thought and stemming from various conceptualist philosophies. What Plotinus is saying is that there is one identical form, or intelligible determination, which exists in soul in one way and in intellect in another. This is an "ontology of knowledge" based on his theory of *logos* and its emanation. There is no notion of some "conceptual order" standing as object between soul and being. Of course, not every theory of "logical distinctions" is conceptualist. Plotinus' account is not entirely different from a theory which attributes logical distinctions to the "*way* in which" something is understood, in contrast to "*that* which" is understood. But if a given "that" is identical on both levels, Plotinus cannot allow undifferentiated unity to correspond on Intellect's level to "thats" which are separable in the soul.

---

[9] VI. 7 [38], 40, 15-18; *cf*. 41, 10-14; V. 6 [24], 1, 12-13, 23-24; 2, 6-7. *Cf*. also VI. 9 [9], 6, 42-54; V. 1 [10], 4, 31-38; V. 3 [49], 10, 23-26; 44-47.

Distinction in Hypostasis

Even though "not divided except in thought" says something about the thing itself, it implies that another sort of division in the thing is possible. Things in the sensible world are of course *more* divided, and Plotinus uses this fact to explain our propensity to divide the intelligible world in our *epinoia*.[10] But is anything in the intelligible world itself distinguishable in some way other than in thought?

In VI. 6 [34], speaking of "priority and posteriority" rather than "division," Plotinus contrasts "prior in *epinoia*" with "prior in subsistence (hypostasis)" (9, 11-14). In his criticism of the Gnostics, he argues that, if they mean their two intellects, "intellect knowing" and "intellect knowing it knows," to be "other in *epinoia*," then they are "abandoning the idea of a plurality of hypostases" (II. 9 [33], 1, 41-42). It is safe to infer from these passages that the three – no more no less – hypostases he is defending against the Gnostics are not just distinct in *epinoia*. He surely would not call them "divided" or "separate," but at least they are "other in *hypostasis*." They are distinct, not as "parts" of one "whole," but as wholes, one of which stands as image of the other.[11]

---

[10] V. 9 [5], 5. 9-11; *cf.* VI. 5 [23], 2, 1-6; VI. 2 [43], 7, 6-24.

[11] The contrast between *kat' epinoian* and *kath' hypostasin* seems to have originated with the Stoics (Diogenes Laertius, *Lives* VII, 135; Proclus, *Commentary on Euclid*, Definition I, Friedlein p. 89; Arius Didymus, *Epitome*, Frag. 20, *Doxographi Graeci* # 458). The Stoics' *hypostasis* is body of course, and their use of *kat' epinoian* smacks of conceptualism and even of aggressive anti-Platonism; it throws little light on Plotinus' use. Still, controversy has a way of creating a common vocabulary, and this may be what happened with Stoics and Platonists. The actual expression "three hypostases" appears only in the title of V. 1 [10]. Plotinus himself calls them "three natures" in V. 1, 8, 27. Even though the titles are not by Plotinus, it is reasonable to suppose he knew and gave tacit approval to the titles being used by his disciples, or at least to the way of talking they represent. If not that, at least the titles that "came to prevail" (*Life*, 4, 17-19) represent the disciples' common understanding of the master's teaching. Two articles in *The Structure of Being: a Neoplatonic Approach*, ed. R. Baine Harris (Albany, N.Y.: State University of New York Press, 1982) debate a fine point: whether the One should be called "quasi-hypostasis" or "hypostasis." They are "Some Logical Aspects of the Concept of Hypostasis in Plotinus," by John P. Anton, pp. 24-33, and "The One, or God, is not Properly 'Hypostasis': a Reply to Professor John P. Anton," by John N. Deck, pp. 34-39.

Causal Order

There is another way in which we "divide *ousia*" that deserves brief mention. It occurs when we are seeking to understand, not the intelligible itself, but the sensible world, and how the intelligible is embodied there. Following the lead of Plato's *Timaeus*, we are apt to suppose that this embodiment results from deliberation and adapting means to preconceived ends.[12] We think this way because our way of understanding the sensible world consists in constructing causal syllogisms which express why things are the way they are:

> You can explain the reason why the earth is in the middle, and round, and why the ecliptic slants as it does; but it is not because you can do this that things are so there [i.e., in the intelligible world]....It is as if the conclusion was there before the syllogism which showed the cause, and did not follow from the premises; the world order is not the result of following out a train of logical consequences and purposive thought: it is before consequential and purposive thinking; for this comes later, reasoning and demonstration and conviction (V. 8 [31], 7, 37-44).

In VI. 7 [38], 1-3, Plotinus undertakes to rewrite the *Posterior Analytics* and eliminate the causal syllogism, thus adapting it to intuitive intellect. The intelligible – the intelligible man, or horse, or what have you – must contain within itself and be identical with its "cause" (*aitia*, 1, 57), its "why" (*dia ti*, 2, 6-8). In contrast with the sensible, in the intelligible "the essence (ousia) and the what-is-being (to ti en einai) and the why (to dioti) are one thing" (3, 21-22; *cf.* VI. 8 [39], 14 & 17). When he speaks of "cause" here, Plotinus is thinking primarily of the end, since he is excluding deliberation from Intellect, but he means cause in general. He points out one example – the

---

[12] See espec. VI. 7 [38], c. 1 and *cf.* V. 8 [31], 7, 1-9.

eclipse–where cause and thing are the same "even here" (2, 11-12), and an eclipse is not defined by its end.

By thus dividing the "One-many," soul is deployed for the creation of the universe but also for that utterance by which the individual soul, trapped in that universe, will effect its escape.

Utterance and the Embodied Soul

So far the multiplicity we have been examining is the multiplicity that appears in *logismos* as such. This multiplicity in the soul's activity argues that in being as well Soul is less unified than Intellect. If Intellect is the One-many Plotinus finds in the *Parmenides*, then Soul is the One-and-many he also finds there, in 155E.[13] The Forms in Soul are "unfolded and separated."

What constitutes Soul as distinct from Intellect would seem to be this multiplicity in being rather than Soul's propensity to reason. Neither the World Soul nor human souls that have departed this life engage in reasoning.[14] Apparently, though, their intuitive grasp of the intelligible world is not so simple and unified as that of Intellect itself–not that they go over it part by part, but their timeless vision of the whole is by multiple acts "all together."[15] This would seem to be consistent with Soul's greater multiplicity in being. It also explains how Soul in general is able to convey

---

[13] See V. 1 [10], 8, 27; *cf.* IV. 2 [4], 2, 53-55.

[14] On the World Soul, see, besides the passages cited in note 12, IV. 3 [27], c. 10; IV. 4 [28], cc. 9-12. On the individual soul, see IV. 3, 18 and IV. 4, 1. These souls do not use "speech" (phone) either. That would seem to go without saying, but Plotinus is prepared to suppose that they are not totally disembodied but have some sort of celestial body. Even on that hypothesis "there would be none of that talk there which they engage in here because of needs or over doubtful and disputed points." Instead they would know "by intuition what passes from one to another" (IV. 3, 18, 13-19). This incidental remark strikes me as throwing so little light on the nature of language that I have relegated it to a footnote, despite the nature of this study. Some find it more significant; see, for instance, Charles-Saget, *L'architecture du divin*, p. 303.

[15] IV. 4 [28], 1, 20 ff.; *cf.* IV. 3 [27], 18, 10-13.

logos to the multiple and divided world of bodies[16] – a thing, be it noted, that my soul is presently doing with no more conscious planning than is found in the World Soul. And once the human soul has entangled itself with a body, it is through this multiplicity in being that it engages in *logismos*, and ultimately in the dialectic by which it escapes this entanglement. You can even call the disembodied souls themselves "rational" (logistikoi), if by that you mean that they have the capacity to reason when that becomes necessary (IV. 3 [27], 18, 8-9).

What then of speech? It is plainly the outward expression of inward reasoning. As Plato's "inner dialogue of the soul" suggests, there appears to be some sort of point by point correspondence between the process of reasoning and the process of uttering such reasoning in speech. Both are spread out in time. Both involve what Plotinus calls *diexodos*, "discursiveness."[17] The *logos* in our soul, Plotinus tells us, enters our conscious awareness when it is received into our imagination, apparently as inner speech. Does this mean that reasoning is simply that inner speech – words heard with the imagination instead of with the ear? Of if not this, is it perhaps just word-meanings understood? The uttered *logos*, Plotinus tells us, is "broken up" into multiplicity when compared to the *logos* in soul. Is this contrast only with the *logos* which constitutes soul's being, or is there greater multiplicity in speech than in *logismos*, soul's activity?

Plotinus does not raise this question directly, but I believe we can infer an answer from what he says about the sciences in the soul and their "parts." As we saw above, each of these parts – the individual considerations (theoremata) a science comprises – contains the whole science "potentially."[18]

---

[16] On this, see especially III. 7 [45], 11, 19-43.

[17] V. 9 [5], 7, 9-11; V. 8 [31], 6, 7-12; VI. 6 [34], 16, 23; VI. 2 [43], 21, 27-28; *cf.* III. 7 [45], 11, 22-25.

[18] IV. 9 [8], 5, 8 ff.; III. 9 [13], 2, 1-4; IV. 3[27], 2, 50-55.

In his treatise "On the Oneness of All Souls" (IV. 9 [8]), Plotinus develops this theme at some length in chapter 5:

> ...knowledge is a whole, and its parts are such that the whole remains and the parts derive from it...that which has been brought into readiness because it is needed is an actualized part, and this part is put in front, but the other parts follow as unnoticed possibilities, and all are in that part. And perhaps this is the meaning of "whole" and "part" here: in the whole, all the parts are in a way actual at once; so each one which you wish to bring forward for use is ready; but in the part only that which is ready for use is actual; but it is given power by a kind of approach to the whole. But one must not think of it as isolated from all other rational speculations (theoremata); if one does, it will no longer be according to art or knowledge, but just as if a child was talking. If then it is according to knowledge, it contains also all the other parts potentially...and the geometer in his analysis makes clear that the one proposition contains all the prior propositions by means of which the analysis is made and the subsequent propositions which are generated from it (8-26).

Here we have a contrast between merely mouthing words like a child and speaking from science. The difference is not just that the scientist has something going on in his mind. Inner reasoning participates in the unity of the science itself in a way that outer speech does not. Even inner speech, if by that you mean the mere sequence of imagined sounds, falls short of this unity. Of course not all reasoning issues from science. Some of it leads up to science, or at least potentially leads up to science; but even this is the beginning of recollection. It could hardly be that if it did not at least point to a unity transcending utterance.

The unity of science is prior to the multiplicity of its "parts." For this reason Plotinus flatly denies that the sciences, even human sciences "in this world," are a collection of "theorems" and "propositions."[19] We may *utter* them piecemeal in a series of propositions. But even the sum total of such propositions does not constitute the science unless brought to a unity they cannot possibly have as uttered speech.

Plotinus was aware of an alternate theory, the Stoic, which reserved the name "proposition" (axioma) for the *understood meaning* of a statement – what it "says" (the *lekton*) – rather than for the utterance which is its sign.[20] He will have none of such a theory. Propositions, he says, are just "writing" (*grammata*, I. 3 [20], 5, 18), and the dialectician will no more concern himself with propositions and syllogisms, and with logic in general, than he will with learning to write (*ibid.* 4, 18-20). Logic, therefore, emerges at a lower level than we might have expected; not that of reasoning as such, but of *uttered* reasoning. What corresponds within to the uttered proposition is a "movement of the soul" either affirming or denying (5, 20-21).[21] We will examine this rejection of the Stoic *lekton* in more detail in the next chapter, when we examine the way in which "saying" is and is not found in Intellect itself. It is in this context that Plotinus makes clear why he relegates logic to grammar school, and why he cannot view *logismos* as the mere understanding of word meanings.

---

[19] V. 8[31], 4, 48-51. The Loeb has "proportions" instead of "propositions" for *protaseis* here – a misprint.

[20] Sextus Empiricus, *Adversus Mathematicos* VII, 38; VIII, 10 12 and 70. See also Aulus Gellius, *Noctes Atticae* XVI, 8, in Von Arnim, *Stoicorum Veterum Fragmenta* II, 194. In Plotinus, see V. 5 [32], 1, 38-39.

[21] Despite his opposition to the Stoics on this issue, Plotinus may have borrowed the phrase "kinemata tes psyches" from them. See *Adversus Mathematicos* VII, 242.

CHAPTER V
INTELLECTUAL "SAYING"

What we have said up to now would suggest that to "say," whether in uttered speech or in inner reasoning, is an activity proper to Soul. Yet we have seen that Intellect also "says," even though, unlike Soul, it "is" what it "says." In fact, when he is arguing that the One cannot have *noesis*, Plotinus makes it seem that the very nature of *noesis* is to be an act of "saying," even "predicating." This is startling, since he usually describes *noesis* in terms of "seeing" rather than "saying." And we have just seen him denying that even "our sciences" are made up of "propositions." How then can Intellect be "predicating"?

Yet we find him arguing in VI. 7 [38], 38, 9-25, that the Good cannot have *noesis* of itself unless it knows "I am the Good," and thus "predicates" goodness of itself (which it of course cannot do without first distinguishing itself from goodness). A similar argument appears in V. 3 [49], 10, 32-42, but in terms of unity rather than goodness, and of "saying" rather than "predicating":

> For if it directed its gaze to a single object without parts, it would be without thought or word: for what would it have to say about it, or to understand? For if the absolutely partless had to speak of itself, it must, first of all, say what it is not; so

50

that in this way too it would be many in order to be one. Then, when it says "I am this," if it means something other than itself by "this," it will be telling a lie; but if it is speaking of some incidental property of itself, it will be saying that it is many or saying "am am" or "I I."....Therefore the thinker must apprehend one thing different from another and the object of thought in being thought must contain variety.[1]

Having got Intellect to "say" and "predicate," Plotinus appears to lose all restraint. He introduces "movement" into Intellect, and once movement is there, he allows Intellect to "unfold" its content and even "wander" through that content (VI. 7 [38], 13, 28ff.) on an excursion he at one point calls *diexodos* (line 48), a term he usually reserves for the discursiveness of reasoning.[2] What has happened? Have we mounted by dialectic all the way to the intuitive level only to bring *logismos* along with us? In a sense we have, but in a sense that must be made more precise. He tells us in VI. 2 [43], 21, 32-34:

As a universal rule, whatever anyone might come upon by *logismos* as existing in nature, these same things he will find existing in intellect without *logismos*.

But if without *logismos*, what is all this talk of "unfolding" and "wandering," or "predicating" for that matter? One of the things that makes reasoning reasoning would seem to be movement from one point to another. As we saw above, even predication can be seen as a sort of movement – the returning to unity of what has become twofold. So the question would seem

---

[1] *Cf. ibid.* 13, 23-28: "*noesis*...turns inward to an intellect which is obviously multiple; for even if it only says 'I am existent' (on), it says it as a discovery, and says it plausibly, for existence (to on) is multiple: since if it concentrated its gaze on itself as something simple and said 'I am existent,' it would not attain either itself or existence. For it does not mean something like a stone by existence, when it is speaking the truth, but says many things in one word."

[2] See note 20 of Chapter Two. *Cf.* III. 8 [30], 8, 30-38; V. 8 [31], 6, 1-9; VI. 2 [43], 21; V. 3 [49], 11, 1-16.

to be, how can one introduce movement into Intellect without compromising its eternity, immutability, and superior unity?

In a paper he delivered in 1969, Professor Armstrong expressed the view that you cannot do so; that:

> ...the accounts which Plotinus gives of the eternal life of Intellect are not fully coherent, and in particular that he is not always successful in confining his description of it within the limits imposed by the concept of non-durational eternity, on which he so strongly insists.[3]

I do not believe Professor Armstrong means that, in moments of absent-mindedness, Plotinus was apt to forget that Intellect was supposed to be timeless and immutable. Rather, Plotinus' descriptions of Intellect in movement, with the movement of intellectual life, would be "impoverished" (p. 73) if you continued to insist that this life must be timeless and immutable. If we set aside questions of taste (Professor Armstrong admits that Plotinus does not share his own preference for the life of becoming), "impoverished" cannot mean less pleasing esthetically or emotionally. It can only mean diminished in meaning, or entirely deprived of it. So the question is, can you meaningfully talk about "movement" in a timeless and immutable Intellect?

It was Plato who first asked "can we really be so easily persuaded that movement, life, soul and thought are not to be found in what is perfectly real?" (*Sophist* 249A, Cornford). Whatever Plato may have meant by that,

---

[3] "Eternity, Life and Movement in Plotinus' Account of *Nous*," in *Le Néoplatonisme* (Paris: Centre National de la Recherche Scientifique, 1971), p. 74. Professor Armstrong has always been able to find inconsistency in Plotinus' writings to a degree that is simply inconceivable to me. Surely allowing Plotinus the presumption of consistency is not mere charity; it is plain common sense. Even were he incapable of developing consistent views on subjects that must have occupied his mind virtually every day of his philosophic life, he was surrounded by disciples and colleagues of no mean intelligence, such as Porphyry, who could at least ask respectful questions.

Plotinus takes him to mean that the "supreme genus" movement is found on the level of true being, and that this movement is the movement proper to the life of thought.[4]

Aristotle undertook to rethink the whole notion of "life" in terms not of "movement" but of "act" (energeia). Movement, for him, is an "act" of a sort, but an "imperfect act" on the way to completion, with a potentiality not yet fully actualized. But there can also be "act" without movement, not the inert lack of movement characteristic of bodies at rest, but act fully achieved, "perfect act," the act of thinking,[5] "life most good and eternal" (*Meta* XII, 7, 1072b29).

Plotinus was fully aware of this issue. Faithful, as he supposed, to Plato, he denied that movement must be an imperfect act. As he says in VI. 1 [42], 16, "walking is walking" from the start and at every instant (9-10). The only way you can view it as "imperfect" and requiring time for its completion is by seeing it as having a certain quantity—as being a *bodily* movement (14-19).

It may seem that Plotinus' non-bodily, intelligible movement differs in name only from Aristotle's "perfect act." In fact it differs in one other important respect. Movement has one characteristic which act as such does not have, priority and posteriority within a many, in other words, *order*.

If the many are going to emerge from the One, they cannot come tumbling out like a load of coal. They must come out in some sort of order. Plotinus habitually talks of this order in terms of movement—both the "coming out" of Intellect itself, and the "unfolding" of the forms within

---

[4] VI. 7 [38], 8, 22-32; VI. 2 [43], 7, 1-11; *cf.* V. 6 [24], 6, 18-23; VI. 7, 39, 28-32.

[5] *De Anima* III, 7, 431a5-8; *cf. Phys* III, 2, 201b30-32; *Meta* IX, 6, 1048b18-34.

intellect. But he hastens to remind us we must correct this kind of talk by eliminating all implication of process or time.[6]

Plotinus did not originate the idea of speaking in temporal terms of an eternal relationship. Priority and posteriority does not necessarily mean temporal priority and posteriority. Even Aristotle recognized this.[7] And for centuries the majority of Platonists had been claiming that Plato's account of creation in the *Timaeus* was couched in temporal terms only as a pedagogical device (didaskalias charin), in much the same way as geometers describe the "construction" of a figure in order to exhibit its timeless properties. All the *Timaeus* means is that the world, being a copy, depends on its original for its being.[8]

Whatever merits this has as exegesis, it is not unintelligible. *A fortiori*, if Plotinus' eternal and immutable Intellect eternally depends on the One-Good, both as "source from which" and "good toward which," then one can hardly be faulted for describing it as eternally "coming out" and eternally "turning back" and "being fulfilled." And if the present tense suggests a kind of incompletion, then why not say that it eternally *has* come out, or even *came* out at some eternal instant? The movement within Intellect surely should be understood in the same sense. Plotinus relates the two movements in a famous passage:

---

[6] See note 1 of Chapter Two.

[7] *Categ* 12, 14a26-b23; *Phys* VIII, 7, 260b15-19; *Meta* V, 11, 1018b8-1019a14; IX, 8, 1049b3-1051a3.

[8] This interpretation, along with the phrase "didaskalias charin," receives Aristotle's criticism in *De Caelo* I. 10, 279b32-280a2. Simplicius, in his commentary on this passage (ed. Heiberg, pp. 303, 30-304, 15), attributes the view Aristotle is attacking to Speusippus and Xenocrates, as we would have guessed anyway. Thus, this interpretation goes back at least to the first generation of "Platonists," if not to the Master himself. See Matthias Baltes, *Die Weltentstehung des platonischen Timaios nach den antiken Interpreten*, Philosophia Antiqua Vols. XXX and XXXV (Leiden: Brill, 1976-1978). Plotinus echoes the phrase "didaskalias charin" in IV. 3 [27], 9, 15-16, when discussing the relation of World Soul to Universe. "Logos didaskon" in VI. 7 [38], 35, 28, is not a *verbatim* echo, but is an echo nevertheless, and this time it is Intellect's emanation that is in question.

Therefore this multiple Intellect, when it wishes to think that which is beyond, thinks that itself which is one, but in wishing to attain to it in its simplicity comes out continually apprehending something else made many in itself.[9]

We have already seen that there is priority and posteriority within Intellect; the more universal and unified "makes," and hence is prior to the more particular and multiple. Intellect therefore eternally and timelessly "unfolds itself," or, if you like, "explores its own content," even "wanders through" that content.

It follows, then, that not only the multiplicity which reason separates out, but also the order reason follows in its movement[10] is present on the level of intellect without separation or temporal succession. And what of "predication"? Plotinus is not so explicit on this, but since predication is the unifying of what has become multiple, it would seem to be part of Intellect's "return" to the One, just as the "going out" is plurification. This would explain why Plotinus seems to equate self-*noesis* with self-predication, and both of these with "seeking" and "need," in the passages where such things are denied of the One. Intellect's "need" to find predicates for itself is Plotinus' way of accounting for what I referred to above as the "Platonic" multiplicity in the object of Intellect. Intellect's "saying" is what generates the world of Forms.

Thus, on the level of Intellect, all that is significant in rational thought is found without the latter's deficiencies. Why then does Plotinus deny so strenuously that "propositions" are found there? If "predication," why not

---

[9] V. 3 [49], 11, 1-4; *cf.* V. 1 [10], 7; VI. 7 [38], 16, 10-24.

[10] This is not, of course, the order that reasoning invariably follows. As the description of dialectic in the *Republic* has shown, reason must ascend to the Good before it can proceed from it. But both these movements are grounded on the same order in the intelligibles themselves. In VI. 6 [34], Plotinus attempts to determine the priorities in Intellect, and specifically whether the Intelligible Numbers are prior to the Forms. There he distinguishes what "we" put later "in our *epinoia*" from what is later in itself, and suggests means for discovering through reasoning what is the true priority (10, 38-51).

propositions? Are they not the uttered image of the *logos* in the soul, as it, in turn, is the image of Intellect? Yet we have already seen that "even in this life" the sciences in the soul are not made up of "propositions." And this remark was meant to show that *a fortiori* propositions are not found in Intellect.

I do not believe Plotinus would have made such a point of this were it not for the Stoic understanding of propositions. The Stoic proposition (axioma) is their basic unit of rational discourse and of logic. For Plotinus, as we saw, the proposition stands on the side of significant utterance rather than of thought signified. Still, this is not his fundamental difference with the Stoics. He can scarcely deny that the propositions one utters or writes have an understood meaning. But the Stoics tended to make thought *nothing but* the understood meaning of language, in other words, to define thought in terms of language.[11]

This isomorphism of thought and language may endear them to some present-day philosophers of logic and language, but it was not likely to endear them to Plotinus. In V. 5, the treatise which is a continuation of V. 8, he remarks that propositions are not the intelligible, but only "say something about things other than themselves" (1, 40). Language may, in its own inferior mode, mirror forth the *logos* in the soul, but that *logos* cannot in turn be the reciprocal mirroring of the proposition. It must mirror forth the superior unity of the Forms in Intellect. It is only thus that the terms of which a proposition is composed can themselves signify these Forms "primarily" or "by priority," as Plato's allegory of the cave teaches. Failing

---

[11] See Sextus Empiricus, *Adversus Mathematicos* VIII, 70; Diogenes Laertius, *Lives* VII, 49. See also A. A. Long, "Language and Thought in Stoicism," in *Problems in Stoicism*, ed. A. A. Long (London: The Athlone Press, 1971), pp. 75-113, esp. pp. 82-84; Andreas Graeser, "The Stoic Theory of Meaning," in *The Stoics*, ed. John M. Rist (Berkeley, CA: University of California Press, 1978), pp. 77-100; Marc Boratin, "L'identité de la pensée et de la parole dans l'ancien stoicisme," *Langages*, n. 65 (1982): 9-21.

this, language remains trapped among the shadows for which the "legislators" originally framed it, in the cave where the Stoic is content to dwell.

In thus rejecting the Stoic view of speech, Plotinus is adhering to the older view of Plato that speech is the mere instrument of thought, or, as Aristotle puts it, that spoken words are the "symbols of affections in the soul," and through them of the things the soul knows (*Peri Herm* 1, 16a4-8). It should go without saying that "things the soul knows" – knows *primarily* – does not mean for Plotinus what it means for Aristotle.

To counteract our temptation to find "propositions" in Intellect itself, Plotinus, in V. 8, 6, suggests that the symbolic drawings found in Egyptian temples better represent the divine order than do "letters, words and propositions." By means of "one particular image of each particular thing," the Egyptian sages (always assumed to have had superior mystic insight) "manifested the non-discursiveness of the Intelligible World." It is hard to tell how seriously Plotinus means such remarks, but one could surely object that the Egyptian sages eliminate discursiveness only by dividing the Forms one from another, "one image for each thing."[12] Whatever its other deficiencies, discursive thought at least succeeds, finally, in overcoming that division by "weaving the Forms together."

If these temple drawings had not been such a handy stick to beat the Stoics with, Plotinus might not have been so taken with them. Still they do serve to illustrate his main point. Unlike propositional utterances, whether spoken or written, they are not spread out in time or in space. So, as images of *logos*, they are not "broken up," at least in this way. The proposition, on the other hand, is an appearance in space and in time, and it unfolds piecemeal. Like sensible things, it is only an imperfect embodiment of the

---

[12] In V. 5 [32] (sequel to V. 8), c. 1, just after denying that the intelligibles are "propositions," he goes on to say: "But if they are going to say that the intelligibles are simple realities, justice by itself and beauty by itself, then...the intelligible will not be a unity or in a unity, but each intelligible will be cut off from the others" (42-44).

unity of which it is the *logos*. It does not even embody the unity of the "sciences in the soul," to say nothing of the unity of Intellect.

CHAPTER VI
TALKING ABOUT THE ONE

Plotinus' reasons for agreeing with Plato's *Parmenides* that "there is no *logos* of the One" are known well enough to require little comment.[1] As we have seen, his stand stems not from some mystical anti-rationalism, but from a thorough-going rationalism which expects any multiplicity in *logos* to be traced out in being as well. It thus forbids us to "make the One twofold, even in thought." Any statement which purports to say what the One is necessarily makes it twofold in thought, subject and alleged attribute, and thus compromises its unity. So such statements are ruled out.

What needs comment is the kind of "talk about the One" Plotinus finds acceptable despite this injunction. In chapter 14 of V. 3 [49], lines 1-8, he draws a distinction between "speaking about" the One/Good (legein peri autou) – which he obviously does quite often – and attempting to "speak it" (legein auto), that is, express it, or "say what it is" (line 7).[2] This you cannot

---

[1] *Parm* 142A, cited in V. 4 [7], 1, 9 and in VI. 7 [38], 41, 37-38; *cf.* VI. 9 [9], 11, 11; V. 5 [32], 6, 12; V. 3 [49], 13, 4; 14, 2.

[2] Frederic Schroeder, in "Saying and Having in Plotinus," refers to speaking the One as "disclosing" it, and speaking about it as "discussing" it (p. 75). But he finds in V. 3, 14, 8-20 a third kind of "speaking" which he calls "declaring" the One (76-80). I have read his arguments and the words he reads in this sense, and I can find no such third way of speaking even implicit there. Ineffable experience, yes; distinct way of speaking, no. I am not even clear in my mind what this "declaring" would consist in. If speech is to relate to the One in some different but

do. In this passage the kind of "speaking about" which he allows is "saying what it is not" – the *via negativa* – but he adds that in saying what it is not, "we speak about it from the things that come after it" (line 8). This remark suggests that not just the *via negativa*, but in general speaking about the One/Good "from the things that come after it" leaves its unity intact. "Legein peri," even though here "peri" takes the genitive case, seems to carry some of the connotations of "talking around" something.

Plato's description of dialectic in the *Republic* leaves the impression that dialectic gives a *logos* not just of every other thing, but of the Good as well (VII, 534B-C). But one could also gather that this *logos* of the Good would consist in showing how all other things derive from it and depend on it for their being and truth. In other words, it would be dialectic as a whole in its achieved form. Similarly, when Plotinus speaks of Intellect coming forth from the Good, turning back to it and being filled, he is surely "speaking about" the Good, and in this sense giving it a kind of *logos* without trying to "speak it."

Naming the One

But we are not out of the woods yet. There is still the question of *naming* the One. A name would appear to say "what a thing is," and the *Parmenides* rules out names along with *logos*. But you can scarcely "talk about" something without naming it. You cannot just point. So Plotinus names the One, even though he might seem to be thereby saying "what it is." The names he applies to the One besides "one" include "source" (arche) and its cognates – notably "cause," "power of all things" and "the first" – and "good." "Beyond *ousia*" he explains as a negative expression rather than a name.[3] He

---

distinctively linguistic way, I do not think it is enough to say simply that speech, like other things, is created and therefore mirrors forth the creator. And as I say, I do not find Plotinus implying any such thing. So if this third mode of speaking really is integral to his thought, I am obviously unable to integrate it into my account.

[3] V. 5 [32], 6, 11-13; V. 3 [49], 13, 2-5.

uses "source" without apology, since it does not pretend to state what the One is, but only how other things derive from it. "One" and "Good" require more careful handling.

First of all, neither of these quasi-names is a "predicate" indicating some "attribute belonging to it." They are just our means of "indicating" (semainein) or "showing" (deloun) it as best we can[4] (the next best thing to just pointing at it). As to the term "one," Plotinus is inclined to take it in a negative sense, as simply denying multiplicity (V. 5 [32], 6, 26-29) or division into parts (VI. 9 [9], 5, 38-42). If we took it as a positive term, it would not serve its purpose: it would conceal rather than show (presumably by deluding us into thinking we were saying what the One is) (V. 5, 6. 29-31).

"Good" can hardly be dismissed as a negative term. But if not, and if it still names the First Principle, how can you escape the implication that you are saying what the First Principle is? Eliminating the propositional form "it is good" or "it is the Good," and instead just saying "the Good" (VI. 7 [38], 38, 4-9) seems like an evasion. How can you call it that, even if only to point at it, if that is not "what it is"? Still, you have gained something by explaining that this is *not* what you mean by calling it the Good. Plotinus does not pursue the issue further than this, but he does say something in another context that might serve as a solution to the difficulty, and will be so used by later neo-Platonists. The Good, he says, is not good for itself; it is the good of other things.[5] "Good" would thus be the counterpart, on the return movement, of "Source" on the outward movement, and you would be describing the First Principle in terms of "what comes after it."

---

[4] V. 5 [32], 6, 23-26; II. 9 [33], 1, 1-8; VI. 7 [38], 38, 4-9.

[5] VI. 9 [9], 6, 39-42; VI. 7 [38], 41, 27-31; *cf.* III. 8 [30], 11, 10-19; I. 8 [51], 2, 2-8; I. 7 [54], 1, 13-23. The last two passages cite with approval Aristotle's definition of the good in *Nic Eth* I. 1, 1094a3 as "that at which all things aim."

"Improper Talk"

We still have to consider a much more puzzling use of language about the One. This is the "improper speech" that appears in the latter half of VI. 8 [39], "On the Freedom and Will of the One." In this treatise we find a number of very positive names applied to the One with the qualifier *hoion* ("sort of," "quasi," "as it were"). It is hard to know what to make of this. As Father Paul Henry remarked in 1931, commentators both ancient and modern, while unanimous in their admiration for its profundity, make almost no use of *Ennead* VI. 8, "discouraged, perhaps, by the difficulties it presents."[6] So far as I can tell, things have not changed much in the half-century since.

Plotinus explains why he uses such terms in chapter 13 of the treatise:

If we must apply these names in our inquiry despite their impropriety, let me say once again that, to speak properly, we must not make it twofold even in thought. But for present purposes, with a view to persuasion, our words must have an aberrant meaning (*paranoeteon en tois logois*; lines 1-5).

Later in the chapter he continues:

We have to allow words which in strict propriety are not permitted, if one who is speaking of It finds himself constrained to use them to indicate It. Each of them should be taken with a "hoion" (47-50).

This apologizes for the expressions, but it does not really explain why they are necessary, or even legitimate, nor does it tell us what the qualification *hoion* signifies. As to this third question, the meaning of a philosophical expression is normally determined by the reasoning that requires its use, and therefore in this case by the answer to the first two

---

[6] "Le problème de la liberté chez Plotin," *Revue néo-scholastique de philosophie*, XIII (1931): 50-79; 180-215; 318-339.

questions. You cannot decide what "hoion" means simply by examining Plotinus' linguistic practice in other contexts. But you obviously have to start there, since he must have some reason for choosing this word in preference to others.

"Hoion" is an adverbial form which can be prefixed parenthetically to any word or phrase and which Plotinus uses elsewhere to signal an analogy. Thus the soul makes a living being "out of a qualified body and a quasi light which it gives of itself" (I. 1 [53], 7, 3-5; *cf.* VI. 4 [22], 3, 22). The "quasi courage" in Intellect is its "immateriality and abiding pure by itself" (I. 2 [19], 7, 6). The soul of the philosopher is "quasi winged" (I. 3 [20], 3, 2). Real beings are the "quasi matter" of dialectic (*ibid.* 5, 12).

None of these analogies is difficult to grasp. They can even be explained in detail, as Plotinus does the light analogy in IV. 3 [27], cc. 22-23. But that is because both terms of the analogy have distinctive features which can be described and compared, even though one term is more familiar to our incarnate minds than the other. But when one term has no "features" at all, and can only be described negatively, how can it be the term of an analogy?

Plotinus had explained in chapter 8 of VI. 8:

In our inability to find things suitable to say about It, we transfer to It the inferior attributes of Its inferiors, and in this way find something to say about It. Yet nothing we found to say could be said of It directly, or even said *about* It in a proper sense (3-8).[7]

This explains what he is trying to do, but does not justify the attempt. You cannot justify what you are doing by pleading you cannot do better. Even if we accept that "our words must have an aberrant meaning," as he says

[7] *Cf.* 18, 52-53: "This is how we must speak of it, in our inability to speak as we would like."

in chapter 13, how can we know that they are not straying off into plain and unredeemed falsehood?

I believe there are indications in the text of Plotinus that point to an answer to all this. First of all, Plotinus tells us in chapter 13 that he is doing this "with a view to persuasion" (peithous charin). He does not enlarge on this here, but elsewhere, when he talks of *peitho*, he is contrasting "persuasion" with "necessity" or "force" (anangke, bia).[8]

By "persuasion" as opposed to "necessity," he does not mean merely probable or rhetorical arguments. Rather, as he explains in V. 3 [49], 6, 9-18, there are arguments which demonstrate by necessity but fail to convince "us" because these arguments are on the level of "pure intellect," whereas "we" are on the level of soul. We want something in addition to necessity; we want to be persuaded. Persuasion comes from "contemplating the archetype as if in an image" (17-18).

Such arguments, arguments which move from image to archetype, are meant to be more than just probable. In fact, they are the only sort of argument likely to recommend themselves to one unconvinced of the Platonic theory of knowledge. But because Plotinus is sure that we can arrive at a direct grasp of the Forms themselves through "pure intellect," they are not his favorite arguments. Even as elements in human *logismos*, they have second-class status and are just concessions to human weakness. One is reminded of Spinoza apologizing for letting an *a posteriori* argument intrude into the respectable company of proofs for the existence of God.

---

[8] See I. 2 [19], 1, 52-54; VI. 4 [22], 4, 5; VI. 5 [23], 11, 5-7; VI. 7 [38], 40, 1-5; V. 3 [49], 6, 9-18. Bréhier, in the Introduction to his edition of the *Enneads*, p. xxv, suggests that the contrast is an echo of Plato's *Laws* X, 903A-B, which contrasts "compelling by argument" (logois) with "persuading by argument." This in turn would seem to be echoing what Plato had said in Book IV about the laws–that they should "mix persuasion with necessity" in moving citizens to observance (722B-C).

In talking about the One we are, of course, *above* the level of pure intellect. We may have a direct grasp of the intelligible, but we have no direct grasp of the One which would enable us to make it the subject of a rational argument. Instead, the arguments that precede chapter 13 of VI. 8 are arguments based on its absolute unity and transcendence as established by the *via negativa*. Plotinus is right; they are singularly unpersuasive as they attempt to show the One's "freedom" and "voluntary" existence,[9] not least because they appear to be smuggling some positive content into the conclusion. Even if this is just an appearance, it shows that "our" minds want to give some positive meaning to "voluntary," and even to "free." And so, to persuade our minds, we begin in chapter 13 to encounter a proliferation of positive statements about the One. Since the One is being "contemplated in its image," such statements will inevitably need qualification by a "hoion" if they can be made at all.

But how *can* they be made? The solution I am going to propose is based on the fact that Plotinus is not applying just any sort of predicate to the One. He is attributing quasi-*acts* to it – self-directed acts. He himself indicates as much in lines 5-10 of chapter 13 itself. If we examine his actual practice in the remainder of the treatise we find him attributing the following quasi-acts to the One, in addition to "act" in general (7, 47; 13, 56; 16, 15 & 25): quasi-life (7, 51; 15, 25); quasi-volition (13, 6, 27 & 56; 18, 49); quasi-desire (15, 5) or -love of self (16, 13); quasi-looking upon self (16, 21); quasi-making of self (16, 21; 20, 27); quasi-intellect (16, 16) or quasi-"intellect which is not intellect" (18, 21); and quasi-"waking and superintellection (hypernoesis)" (16, 32-33).[10]

---

[9] For an analysis of these arguments, see Henry, "Le problème de la liberté," pp. 320-330; on the transition to "persuasion" see pp. 330-331.

[10] He refers to "hoion hypostasis" (7, 47; 15, 6: "hoion hypostasin kai hoion hypokeimenon"; 20, 10) and "hoion ousia" (7, 52; 13, 7 & 27), but only to say that the One's "quasi-subsistence"

He stresses affective acts over cognitive ones for the obvious reason that VI. 8 is discussing the "freedom" and "voluntariness" of the One. It takes its start with the Aristotelian concepts of "the voluntary" (to hekousion) and "what is in our control" (to eph hemin).[11] This volitional aspect of the One, and of Intellect for that matter, appears nowhere else in the *Enneads*, whereas in other places Plotinus attributes something suspiciously like *noesis* to the One. And in chapter 6 of VI. 8, after a long analysis of what "to hekousion" and "to eph hemin" must be in their purest and most perfect state, he concludes that at this level, the level of Intellect, "willing" (boulesis) is identical with *noesis* (line 41).

For these reasons it seems reasonable to concentrate on what it can mean to attribute a quasi-*noesis* to the One. In addition, Plotinus has argued to exclude *noesis* from the One not only on the general principle that excludes any predicate, but specifically in terms of what makes *noesis noesis*. If despite this we can determine what it means to attribute to the One a "quasi-waking and superintellection," we will be coming as close as we ever will to the meaning of "improper talk" about the One.

Unquestionably the One is an "archetype,"[12] and Intellect is its "image."[13] So there are "traces" of the One in Intellect.[14] But is this enough to justify talking as if the One in turn were quasi-intellectual? If we regard

---

or "-essence" is identical with its act. In 11, 20 "hoion ousia" appears in an account of the wrong-headed thinking that leads us astray.

[11] *Nic Eth* III. See Henry, "Problème de la liberté," pp. 186-193. Bréhier, in his *Notice* to VI. 8, argues that the treatise was intended to refute a Gnostic view that, since the First Principle exists "for no reason," it exists "by chance." This would explain why the contrast "not as it chanced, but as He willed" recurs as a theme throughout the later chapters of the treatise.

[12] VI. 9 [9], 11, 45; V. 1 [10], 6, 33; III. 8 [30], 11, 20; VI. 8 [39], 18, 27.

[13] V. 4 [7], 2, 26; VI. 9 [9], 11, 44; V. 1 [10], 7, 1; VI. 7 [38], 40, 19; VI. 8 [39], 18, 27.

[14] III. 8 [30], 11, 19-22; VI. 7 [38], 17, 13 & 39; 18, 1-5.

Intellect as *coming from* the One, and on this account infer that the One, its Source, must have something quasi-intellectual about it, we run up against an insuperable objection, it seems to me. Intellect becomes intellect precisely by *differentiating itself* from the One and thus becoming the multiple thing that Intellect must necessarily be. How then can its source have anything even quasi-intellectual about it?

If Plotinus' way of talking has any philosophical basis at all, this must be not the "going forth," but the "return." Of course these are not successive events, but different aspects of one eternal relationship. In his description of Intellect's going forth we have even seen Plotinus splitting that movement in two and inserting the return in between without any apparent feeling of awkwardness. Intellect goes forth and turns back to the One to comprehend it, but failing this, it falls back into multiplicity and generates the world of Forms. Still these two movements, going out and turning back, have to be distinguished, since one is the cause of Intellect's multiplicity and the other of its unity. The causal relationship to the One differs as well – "source from which," "good towards which" – efficient and final cause.

It seems to me that, if the One must be regarded as quasi-intellectual, this must be because it is the Good, the final cause towards which Intellect moves in the act of *noesis*.[15] When Plotinus discusses *noesis* as the *energeia* of Intellect, he gives evidence that he has pondered Book *Lambda* of Aristotle's *Metaphysics* long and deeply. Even when he concludes that the One cannot have *noesis*, he does so on what might be called "Aristotelian" grounds. Aristotle approaches the whole issue from the standpoint of act and final

---

[15] "This is what thinking (noein) is, a movement towards the Good in its desire of the Good" (V. 6 [24], 5, 8-9). *Cf.* III. 8 [30], 11, 7-9, 22-25; VI. 7 [38], 35, 20-27; V. 3 [49], 10, 50-51; 11, 1-6. In fact all activity (energeia) is directed towards the Good (V. 6, 5, 18; *cf.* I. 7 [54], 1, 1-11). See also René Arnou, S. J., *Le désir de Dieu dans la philosophie de Plotin*, 2nd ed. révue et corrigée (Rome: Gregorian University Press, 1967). This classic Plotinian study first turned my thoughts in the direction they have followed on this issue. Father Arnou is not to blame for where these thoughts ended up.

68

causality. The Supreme *Arche* must be absolutely simple (XII. 7, 1072a30-34; V. 5, 1015b11-16) and the Highest Good (XII. 7, 1072a26-36). It cannot be this if it is not identical with its act of *noesis* (XII. 7, 1072b26-31), or if this act is directed at anything beyond itself (chapter 9).

Plotinus accepts Aristotle's premise, but argues that even if Intellect is identical with its act and that act is entirely self-directed, it cannot on that account be called absolutely simple and the Highest Good. Here, as in his denial that the One has a *logos*, we see Plotinus' realism of *logos* at work. But this time it is not just the multiplicity of *logos* which is at issue; it is the causal order of *logos*. Aristotle has asked a question it is absurd to ask: what is it that makes the Good good? He cannot retrieve his blunder by hastening to assure us that the act making the Good good is totally self-directed. The Good must be good simply by itself, with no "need" of *noesis* or any other act.[16]

Still, Plotinus seems to have been impressed by Aristotle's question: "If it thinks nothing, what is there here of dignity (hoste ti semnon)? It is just like one who sleeps" (XII. 9, 1074b17-18). The reference to "quasi-waking and superintellection" in VI. 8 gives evidence of this.[17] Whether or not Aristotle's question was in his mind when he wrote V. 4 [7], what he says in chapter 2 answers it:

> ...but it is not like something senseless (hoion anaistheton); all things belong to it and are in it and with it. It is completely able to discern itself; it has life in itself and all things in itself, and its thinking of itself (katanoesis autou) is itself, and exists by a kind of immediate self-consciousness (hoionei

---

[16] V. 4 [7], 2, 13-15; VI. 9 [9], 6, 43-50; V. 6 [24], 4, 1-5; 5, 1-5; III. 8 [30], 11, 7-25; VI. 7 [38], 37, 1-28; V. 3 [49], 10, 47-53.

[17] For other evidence, see Pierre Hadot, "Etre, vie, pensée chez Plotin et avant Plotin," *Les sources de Plotin*, pp. 113-115.

synaisthesei), in everlasting rest and in a manner of *noesis* different from the *noesis* of Intellect (15-19).

The shockingly positive character of this, even with the *hoion* and the *hoionei*, is not, I think, the most significant thing about it. Rather it is the argument it implies – that the One must have "quasi self-consciousness" in order not to be "like something senseless." This is conceding too much to Aristotle; it suggests a "need."[18] He never argues this way again. Even when he cites Aristotle's question explicitly in III. 8 [30],[19] his only answer is to deny that the One has "need" of *noesis*. But this does not prevent him from attributing to the One "a sort of simple apprehension directed toward itself" (haple tis epibole pros hauto) in VI. 7 [38], 38, 25-26, or from using the *hoion* phrases we encounter in VI. 8 [39]. On what grounds?

I submit the only grounds possible are that the One must have, without the "need" of *noesis*, that which Intellect reaches out for in that movement towards the Good called *noesis*. And not only reaches out for, but somehow *attains*. "With that in it which is not intellect," Intellect is united with the One.[20]

When Plotinus is describing the "coming forth" of Intellect in III. 8 [30], 8, he makes a remark that is somewhat untypical. It would have been "better for Intellect" not to have come forth (35-36). Plainly Intellect would not *be* at all if it had not pluralized itself into Intellect. But, on Plotinus' own principles, this multiplicity can hardly be regarded as an *improvement* on the

---

[18] He explains the fallacy in VI. 7 [38], 37, 24-28: "An intellect that does not know is ignorant. If knowing belongs to a thing's nature, it is ignorant if it does not do it. But when a thing has no function, why supply it with a function and then speak of it in terms of privation when it does not perform that function? That is like calling it 'unmedical.'"

[19] "For certainly it will be either a thinking being or something unthinking. Well, if it is thinking it will be an intellect, but if it is unthinking, it will be ignorant even of itself, so that what will be grand about it (hoste ti semnon)?" (9, 13-16).

[20] V. 5 [32], 8, 23; *cf.* "intellect which is not intellect" in VI. 8.

unity of the One which preceded it. It is a falling away. If, "before" falling away and translating the One into its own multiple terms, Intellect was in contact with the One itself (VI. 7 [38], 15, 16-24; V. 3 [49], 11, 1-16), then it would plainly have been better if, *per impossibile*, it had not fallen away from that unity. But then there would have been no Intellect–just the One itself. So *that* must be what the One has by way of "quasi superintellection" and "a certain simple self-apprehension."[21]

In VI. 8, we are "speaking of the archetype from the image." Since the One is the term of Intellect's act, and has, or rather is, what Intellect is seeking through *noesis*, it seems legitimate to refer to this as a "quasi-waking and superintellection" or "Intellect which is not intellect, so to speak." In the same way we can refer to the One as "quasi-self-loving," "quasi-voluntary," "quasi-free."[22] Do these "hoions" indicate an analogy as they do elsewhere in Plotinus? He himself uses the term "analogia," both as a way of conceiving something,[23] and as a mode of argument which must be used critically,[24] but

---

[21] *Cf.* the first chapter of V. 6 [24], an extended refutation of Aristotle's theory of the *noesis noeseos*, where Plotinus uses the "escape" metaphor to point towards the One/Good. He represents Intellect's movement toward self-*noesis* as an "escape from being two" which is not completely successful. Even what knows something other than itself "wants to know itself" and thus escape duality. The self-knower "escapes further" from duality, but cannot escape altogether and remain a knower. I believe what I have been saying also gives more point to Plotinus' enigmatic remark in VI. 9 [9], 6, 52-55, that we "must not rank the One on the side of the thinker but rather of the *noesis*, for *noesis* does not think but is the cause of thinking in some other thing." It also helps somewhat to clarify that all but opaque lesson he reads to the Peripatetics in VI. 7, 40, in an effort to "mix persuasion with necessity" for their benefit–surely one of the outstanding failures of philosophic exposition.

[22] Lest this whole account seem spun out *a priori* and with no attention to the text of VI. 8, I submit that the following passages from the latter part of that treatise embody this line of thought: 13, 11-40; 15, 1-10; 16; 17, 24-27; 18, 1-7. Other passages such as 18, 18-41 argue from derivation, and hence seemingly from procession rather than return. But derivation means more than just "coming out"; it includes the turning back by which Intellect becomes Intellect in act.

[23] II. 2 [14], 2, 8-13; III. 6 [26], 1, 33-38; VI. 3 [44], 1, 6-7; 5, 1-3; I. 8 [54], 14, 10-13.

[24] I. 2 [19], 1, 36-39; VI. 1 [42], 16, 19-25.

he does not use the term in VI. 8. I do not know if he would have accepted it.[25]

He tells us that we learn about the One "by analogies, negations, knowledge of what comes after it, and certain steps upward" (VI. 7 [38], 36, 6-8). But the only analogues of the One he identifies by that name are the "mathematical one" and the "point" (VI. 9 [9], 5, 41-46), and the "center" of a "circle" which is the soul (*ibid.* 8, 11-16). As a Platonist with neo-Pythagorean sympathies, Plotinus views these mathematical analogies as more than the mere literary embellishments we might take them for. Still they do not seem to be on all fours with "quasi-superintellection." I say this partly because the latter is an *act* directed to the One, but there is another reason as well.

You can establish, on grounds altogether independent of the mathematical analogies, that the one must be uniquely one and be that from/to which the soul relates. You can thus use these analogies consciously as a means of illustrating your conclusions – "draw" the analogies – and even point out, as Plotinus in fact does, in what way they are misleading and in what way appropriate. But there is no way of coming to conceive the One as quasi-intellectual except "through its image." The *via negativa* enables you to exclude certain features of *noesis* from the One, but you cannot – cannot in principle – state what it is about *noesis* that is preserved in the One. Maddeningly, the only appropriate way for Plotinus to describe the One's "life, as it were," is by such exasperating terms as "superintellection" and "intellect that is not intellect."[26]

---

[25] Needless to say, I am using "analogy" in the Greek sense, not the sense it came to have in medieval theology, where it designates any homonymy that is not mere chance homonymy. There would obviously be "analogy" in the medieval sense. The Greeks reserved *analogia* for a similarity that could be expressed in terms of ratios (logoi) – "A is to B as C is to D": – what the medievals called *proportionalitas*.

[26] John M. Rist, in *Plotinus: The Road to Reality*, p. 51, suggests that *epibole* is Plotinus' "favorite word" for the One's inner life, because it appears to avoid the "Aristotelian implications" of *katanoesis* and *hypernoesis*. Modified by the negative term "simple" (haple)

When talking about Intellect, we can get beyond the "persuasive" approach by turning to the pure intelligible itself. Even our *logismos* deals primarily with that as object. But our *logismos* has no resources for rectifying our "incorrect language" about the One other than the *via negativa*. If we want to get beyond this, we must do the same thing Intellect itself does:

> This is how we must speak of It, in our inability to speak of It as we would like. Therefore let the one who has been borne upward toward It by our words, lay hold of It Itself, and he will gaze upon It himself without being able to say what he would like (18, 52-55; 19, 1-3).

The corrective of "incorrect language" about the One is not more talk, but the silence of mystical union, "seeing it in itself, putting aside all *logos*" (*ibid.* 3-4). Even Intellect cannot apprehend the One by "saying" it: "Take away otherness, and it will become one and fall silent" (V. 1 [10], 4, 38-39). This passage from *logos* to silence marks the end of philosophy – not so much its limit as its goal. *Logos* of its very nature is a seeking and points beyond itself. As VI. 8 puts it:

> Why should one ask questions when he has no further advance to make? All inquiry proceeds to a first principle and comes to a halt at just such a point as this (11, 3-5).

The goal of all talk, even the "talk" of Intellect, is silence.

---

and the indefinite "a certain" (*tis*, with almost the force of *hoion*), *epibole* does avoid the *Platonic*, object- and *logos*-related implications of *noesis*; that is what the context of VI. 7, 38 requires with its talk about what the One would "say" or know itself "as." But it does not appear to escape the duality of a self-directed act. That seems to be what Professor Rist means by "Aristotelian implications." And if one supposes that there ought to be some *positive way of putting* what is going on up there in the One, and that *epibole* comes closer to this than *hypernoesis* or *nous ou nous*, then this is surely not Plotinian. For him even "one" is an obstacle to understanding if it masquerades as a positive term. *Epibole* does not reappear among the "hoion" terms in VI. 8, which suggests Plotinus only "favors" it in the context of VI. 7.

CHAPTER VII
CONCLUSION

This has turned out to be more a treatise in metaphysics and philosophic method than in the philosophy of language. I warned that it would, but to readers who expected less of the former and more of the latter I can only apologize and hope they will agree that Plotinus' views could not otherwise have been brought to light. There is no compartment in Plotinus' mind that contains something called his "philosophy of language," as distinct from his metaphysic, any more than there is a compartment containing something called his "epistemology" or his "psychology," as distinct from his metaphysic. I am not so sure there ought to be.

The method I have been using to reconstitute what I take to be Plotinus' theory of language and *logos* has been a hypothetico-deductive one. It is the only one I know how to use when working at the periphery of a philosopher's thought. Assume that his views are on the whole well thought-out and coherent. With that assumption, when you find him saying something not immediately clear in its meaning, ask yourself in the light of his principles why he said it. Having conjectured why, see whether what he says elsewhere is consistent with your hypothesis. If not, the hypothesis must be revised or discarded. Only if no revision or new hypothesis renders him consistent should the assumption of consistency be discarded. The ultimate goal is to construct a system coherent in itself and consistent with all the textual evidence. I believe I have achieved such a system in this study.

I suppose everybody follows this hypothetico-deductive procedure to some extent. The only reason I mention it is that many students of Plotinus seem either too ready to discard the presumption of consistency or reluctant to speak where Plotinus is silent. Sometimes this is because they prefer to account for what Plotinus says by the supposed historical sources of his thought rather than by the exigencies of that thought itself. But just as often it is due to an austere sense of fidelity to the text, so that to some I must seem to be playing fast and loose with that text. I do not think that I have, and I can only say again, I know no other way.

As I said in Chapter Two, two texts appear to be central and thematic to Plotinus' views on language: the texts which describe a descent of *logos* from Intellect to Soul and from Soul to utterance. In these texts, Plotinus tells us what language "says" and how it "says" it. After examining all Plotinus' other remarks which touch upon aspects of this descent, I find them to be consistent and to embody a thought-out and coherent view of language and *logos*. It is even a *surprisingly* coherent view, since almost all the texts, even the "central" ones, are quite tangential to Plotinus' main point of the moment.

But Plotinus' account of language is not just an impressive monument of antiquity. It is an impressive example of what one can make of language by integrating it with an ontology, by viewing language as revelatory of being through the medium of thought. Following Plato's lead, Plotinus was convinced that language "says," or at least ought to "say being." Surely there is some truth to this.

Then how successful is Plotinus' own attempt to make language say being? Specifically, how consistent is it with its Platonic inspiration? And how consistent is it with the philosopher's experience of "giving a *logos*"? I began studying Plotinus many years ago with the understanding that his neo-Platonism might be an impressive achievement in its own right, but it is certainly not the Platonism of Plato. But very early on I had occasion to examine his explanation of *Timaeus* 35A on the "ingredients" of the soul, a text he examines possibly more often than any other. When I had finished, I was left with the surprised reaction: "I am not convinced that is what Plato meant, but if he didn't, what in the world did he mean?" I have not found a convincingly better explanation. This has happened on more than one occasion since.

Plotinus has been called a *Plato dimidiatus*, "Plato diminished by half," that is, a Plato without a political philosophy.[1] A Plato with no interest in the political order is certainly no Plato. Even the *Timaeus* is political. And of course students of Plato have long since given up looking for Plato's "system" in his dialogues despite the fact that, from one end of his writing career to the other, Plato assumes that the intelligible itself is a "system." Since Plotinus, if anyone, has a "system," his Platonism is certainly not the Platonism of the dialogues. But I do not believe one can accuse him of ignoring those dialogues or only using them when they suit his purpose. Nor can you accuse him of infidelity to Plato for creating a system of his own; Plato invites you to.

I began this study by reviewing briefly some of the things Plato says about *logos* in the dialogues. After working out to my own satisfaction what Plotinus thinks on the same subject, I am left with the same old reaction: if Plato did not mean *that*, what *did* he mean? On this, as on many subjects, Plotinus is much closer to the Plato of the dialogues than he gets credit for being.

---

[1] Willy Theiler, "Plotin zwischen Plato und Stoa," *Les sources de Plotin*, p. 67. The phrase comes in for considerable comment in the subsequent discussion of the paper.

But there is one point on which I find his theory sharply at variance with Plato and also, I think, with his own philosophical *praxis*. This is in his concept of the *spoudaios*, that god-like being who has attained *noesis* and is done with *logismos* except to "declare what is in him to another." I do not believe Plotinus means the *spoudaios* to be the counterpart of the Stoic sage. There ought to be a few concrete examples of the *spoudaios* around, and Plotinus must surely have felt himself to be one of them. Yet to the end of his life he was engaged in writing – giving a *logos* – even, apparently, after he had ceased holding conferences. It is hard to believe that he was motivated solely by a desire to "declare what was in him to another." The writings themselves seem to reveal a probing mind seeking deeper insight.

In Plato's ideal republic, the ideally educated philosophers do reach some sort of plateau about the age of fifty, when they at last see all things in relation to the good (VII, 540A). But then their only desire is to continue their pursuit of philosophy to the end of their lives (540B). And this is obviously a collaborative *pursuit*. They are not just teachers, they are seekers as well. So, I submit, was Plotinus, despite his theoretical account. On this point his theoretical account seems to me as far from the Plato of the dialogues as anything he ever wrote.

It is scarcely credible that Plotinus could have engaged in philosophical reflection, discussion and writing for years and not have noticed what he was doing. In fact, he does have a bit more to say about the contemplative life of the *spoudaios* than just his one rather casual remark in the treatise "On Contemplation." One thing he says may throw some additional light on how he conceived his work as a philosopher. His longest sustained discussion of the *spoudaios* appears in the late treatise "On *Eudaimonia*" (I. 4 [46]); it is the *spoudaios* who has achieved *eudaimonia*. In chapter 13 Plotinus addresses the question whether the vicissitudes of chance can hinder the *spoudaios* in his contemplative activity.

He answers by distinguishing between the vision of the Good as a whole (tes tou agathou holou theas), Plato's "greatest study" (megiston mathema, *Republic* VI, 502A), and the investigation of particular points (kath' hekasta). The *spoudaios* might find circumstances an obstacle if he wished to present the results of such investigations, but the *megiston mathema* is always available to him.

It is *logismos* not *noesis* that considers the partial and particular; *noesis* is vision of the whole. I take it then that "the vision of the Good as a whole" is *noesis*, even though, as attaining the Good itself, it goes "beyond *noesis*" as well. If you are "investigating," you are inevitably investigating a "particular point." Plotinus does not exactly say that the *spoudaios* investigates particular points solely for the purpose of communicating them. We might assume that from what he says in the treatise "On Contemplation." It may also be the most likely implication of the passage we are now considering, which is one of his more elliptical remarks.[2] His explicit point is just that circumstances can hinder the communication of what he contemplates. But it is difficult to believe Plotinus would have referred to the activity as "investigation" (zetein kai skepsesthai) if all the *spoudaios* was doing was figuring out what to say in order to "communicate what is in him to another."

The *spoudaios* who undertakes to investigate a particular point for whatever reason would seem to be "working it out" for himself as well as for others. Perhaps we can infer from IV. 3, 30 that this "inner dialog" is the way *noesis* comes to full consciousness even in the *spoudaios*, as I surmised in Chapter One above. On the level of *logismos*, and even in the consciousness of *noesis*, he would then be advancing. Even so, I cannot see how this can be supposed to enhance, or even affect, *noesis* itself. That would seem to be

---

[2] Translators usually supply a phrase or two to bring out what they conceive to be the connection between *zetesas kai skepsamenos* (having researched and investigated) and *propheroi* (presents), and of both to the circumstances of the *spoudaios*. So far as I can make out, the Loeb translation solves the problem by simply omitting *propheroi*.

something you either have as a whole or do not have at all. And surely it is *noesis* which is the whole object of the philosopher's pursuit "in relation to himself." Once he has attained it he has no further advance to make in his "vision of the Good as a whole." Not only that, but philosophy itself would seem to have no further advance to make in this "megiston mathema." Only an endless parade of "learners" down the centuries, each in turn advancing to *noesis*, generation by generation, like the eternal species of Aristotle. This gives point to Plotinus' insistence that he is not being "original," and to his conviction that the truth can be found beneath the most "enigmatic" utterances of the "ancients."

This is no minor point. If Plotinus' account of *noesis*, both in itself and in its relation to *logismos*, proves to be untrue to the human experience of knowing, then out it must go. And that may just prove fatal to the system as a whole. More than this. I happen to think that Plotinus' account of *noesis* is the only way to make coherent sense of the Platonic theory of reminiscence, and I do not think that a Platonic theory of knowledge can stand without a theory of reminiscence or its equivalent.

If we demythologize the concept of reminiscence and eliminate what pertains to sensuous memory – remembering something "previously seen" – we are left with the mere recovering or actualizing of knowledge from within rather than from without. All that remains is to determine the nature of the knowledge relation. This is a matter Plato does not consider, at least in his dialogues. Plotinus is right, I think, to take a hint from Aristotle and see it as a sort of identification between knower and known. But if this is the knowledge relation, and if its object, the intelligible, subsists in itself as the network of Forms Plato describes in the *Sophist*, then the achieved understanding of it becomes just that *noesis* Plotinus describes.

If I am right, then Platonism itself has to go, along with Plotinian *noesis*, and Plotinus has killed it in the way devout disciples frequently do, by making the implicit explicit. Plotinus may have been right to see in Plato an invitation to create a "system," but the only kind of system consistent with our human experience of knowing, it seems to me, is an open-ended one. An intuited network of eternal Forms is not an open-ended system. If a system is open-ended, it develops through *logos*, and the philosophic soul never becomes so free from the trammels of reasoning and of language as Plotinus would like to think. And if Plato is right, and language's function is to "say being," then the being it says would appear not to be Plato's version of being, nor is its way of saying the one Plotinus supposes.

LIST OF WORKS CITED

Anton, John P. "Some Logical Aspects of the Concept of Hypostasis in Plotinus." In *The Structure of Being: a Neoplatonic Approach*. Ed. R. Baine Harris. Albany, NY: State University of New York Press, 1982, pp. 24-33.

Armstrong, A. Hilary. "Eternity, Life and Movement in Plotinus' Account of *Nous*." In *Le néoplatonisme*. Paris: Centre Nationale de la Recherche Scientifique, 1971, pp. 67-74.

_____. "Tradition, Reason and Experience in the Thought of Plotinus." In *Plotino e il Neoplatonismo in Oriente e in Occidente*. Rome: Accademia nazionale dei Lincei, 1974, pp. 171-194.

_____, trans. *Plotinus*, with an English translation by A. H. Armstrong. The Loeb Classical Library. 7 vols. Cambridge, MA: Harvard University Press, 1966-88.

Arnou, René. *Le désir de Dieu dans la philosophie de Plotin*. 2me éd. revue et corrigée. Rome: Gregorian University Press, 1967.

82

Baltes, Matthias. *Die Weltentstehung des Platonischen Timaios nach den antiken Interpreten*. Philosophia Antiqua Vols. XXX and XXXV. Leiden: Brill, 1976-78.

Beutler, Rudolf. See Harder.

Blumenthal, Henry J. "*Nous* and Soul in Plotinus: Some Problems of Demarcation." In *Plotino e il Neoplatonismo in Oriente e in Occidente*. Rome: Accademia nazionale dei Lincei, 1974, pp. 203-219.

_____. *Plotinus' Psychology*. The Hague: Martinus Nijhoff, 1971.

Boratin, Marc. "L'identité de la pensée et de la parole dans l'ancien stoicisme." *Langages*. N. 65 (1982): 9-21.

Bréhier, Emile. *La philosophie de Plotin*. Nouvelle éd. Paris: Vrin, 1961.

_____, ed. and trans. *Plotin. Ennéades*. Texte établi et traduit par Emile Bréhier. 6 vols. in 7. 2me éd. Paris: "Les Belles Lettres," 1954-56.

Charles-Saget, Annick. *L'architecture du divin: mathématique et philosophie chez Plotin et Proclus*. Paris: "Les Belles Lettres," 1982.

Cilento, Vincenzo. *Plotino, Paideia antignostica: Riconstruzione d'un unico scritto da Enneadi III, 8; V, 8; V, 5; II, 9*. Firenze: Felice de Monnier, 1971.

Crome, Peter. *Symbol und Unzulänglichkeit der Sprache.* München: Wilhelm Funk, 1970.

Deck, John N. *Nature, Contemplation and the One.* Toronto: University of Toronto Press, 1967.

_____. "The One, or God, is not Properly 'Hypostasis': a Reply to Professor John P. Anton." In *The Structure of Being: a Neoplatonic Approach.* Ed. R. Baine Harris. Albany, NY: State University of New York Press, 1982, pp. 34-39.

Eon, Alain. "La notion plotinienne d'exégèse." *Revue Internationale de Philosophie,* XXIV (1970): 252-289.

Ferwerda, R. *La signification des images et des métaphores dans la pensée de Plotin.* Groningen: Wolters, 1965.

Graeser, Andreas. "The Stoic Theory of Meaning." In *The Stoics.* Ed. John M. Rist. Berkeley, CA: University of California Press, 1978, pp. 77-100.

Hadot, Pierre. "Etre, vie, pensée chez Plotin et avant Plotin." In *Les sources de Plotin.* Geneva: Fondation Hardt, 1960, pp. 104-157.

Harder, Richard, ed. and trans. *Plotins Schriften,* übersetzt von Richard Harder. Neubearbeitung mit griechische Lesetext und Anmerkungen, fortgeführt von Rudolf Beutler und Willy Theiler. 5 vols. in 11. Hamburg: Felix Meiner Verlag, 1956-60.

84

Henry, Paul. "Une comparaison chez Aristote, Alexandre et Plotin." *In Les sources de Plotin*. Geneva: Fondation Hardt, 1960, pp. 429-449.

_____. "Le problème de la liberté chez Plotin." *Revue Néoscholastique de Philosophie*, XIII (1931): 50-79, 180-215, 318-339.

Lloyd, A. C. "Neoplatonic Logic and Aristotelian Logic." *Phronesis*, I (1956): 58-72, 146-160.

_____. "Non-discursive Thought – an Enigma of Greek Philosophy." *Proceedings of the Aristotelian Society*. New Series LXX (1969-70): 261-274.

_____. "Non-propositional Thought in Plotinus." *Phronesis*, XXXI (1986): 258-265.

Long, A. A. "Language and Thought in Stoicism." In *Problems in Stoicism*. Ed. A. A. Long. London: The Athlone Press, 1971, pp. 75-113.

Moraux, Paul. "La joute dialectique d'après le huitième livre des *Topiques*." In *Aristotle on Dialectic: the Topics*. Ed. G. E. L. Owen. Oxford: Clarendon, 1968, pp. 277-311.

Nedoncelle, Maurice. "Les données auditives et le problème du langage dans l'allégorie de la caverne." *Revue des Sciences Religieuses*, XLIV (1970): 165-178.

Pepin, Jean. "Linguistique et théologie dans la tradition platonicienne." *Langages*. N. 65 (1982): 91-116.

Rist, John M. *Plotinus: The Road to Reality*. New York: Cambridge University Press, 1967.

Ryle, Gilbert. "Dialectic in the Academy." In *New Essays on Plato and Aristotle*. Ed. Renford Bambrough. New York: Humanities Press, 1967, pp. 39-68.

_____. "Dialectic in the Academy." In *Aristotle on Dialectic: the Topics*. Ed. G. E. L. Owen. Oxford: Clarendon, 1968, pp. 69-79.

Schroeder, Frederic M. "Saying and Having in Plotinus." *Dionysius*, IX (1985): 75-84.

Schwyzer, H. R. "'Bewusst' und 'unbewusst' bei Plotin." In *Les sources de Plotin*. Geneva: Fondation Hardt, 1960, pp. 341-390.

Sorabji, Richard. "Myths about Non-propositional Thought." In *Language and Logos: Studies in Ancient Philosophy Presented to G. E. L. Owen*. New York: Cambridge University Press, 1982, pp. 205-314.

Theiler, Willy. "Plotin zwischen Plato und Stoa." In *Les sources de Plotin*. Geneva: Fondation Hardt, 1960, pp. 65-103.

_____. See Harder.

Trouillard, Jean. *La purification plotinienne*. Paris: Presses Universitaires, 1955.

Wallis, Richard. "*NOUS* as Experience." In *The Significance of Neoplatonism*. Ed. R. Baine Harris. Norfolk, VA: International Society for Neoplatonic Studies, 1976, pp. 121-153.

INDEX OF TEXTS CITED

Topics

ARIUS DIDYMUS

AULUS GELLIUS

Noctes Atticae

DIOGENES LAERTIUS

Lives of Eminent Philosophers

PLATO

Cratylus

90

94

Ennead V

100

A

aberrant meaning, 62, 63-64.
Academy, 4 & n.
account, intro, 2, 3, 26, 28-29, 76 78.
acquired habits, 29, 37-38, 38n.
action and passion, 40n.
actuality, 6, 32-35, 46.
Alexander of Aphrodisias, 2n.
analogy 6n, 16-17n, 18, 29 &n, 63, 71 & n.
anamnesis 4, 7 & n, 8-9n, 18-19, 28n, 37, 46, 78.
ancients, 1, 21-22, 78.
Anton, John P., 42n, 81.
apprehension: see *epibole*
Aquinas, St. Thomas, 15n.
arche, intro i-ii, 4 & n, 33, 53-54, 60-61, 67-68, 72.
archetype, 64, 66, 70-71.
Aristotle, intro iii, 2-3, 3n, 4-5, 4n, 5n, 6n, 14, 15-16, 26-27, 26n, 27n, 29, 32, 33 & n, 35, 37-38, 39-40, 52-53, 53n, 56, 61n, 66, 67-69, 70n, 71-72n, 78.
Armstong, A. Hilary, 1n, 6n, 51 & n, 81.
Arnou, René, 67n, 81.
art, 37-38.
axioma, 47, 55.

B

Baltes, Matthias, 53n, 82.
becoming, 13-14, 51-52.
being, 12-15, 15n, 22, 28-29, 31 &nn, 32, 33, 38n, 40-41, 51-52, 59-60, 63, 74-75, 79.
Blumenthal, Henry J., 9n, 25n, 82.
bodies, 11, 25, 30, 40n, 44 & n, 45, 52, 63.
Boratin, Marc, 55n, 82.
Bréhier, Emile, 1n, 64n, 66n, 82.

C

cause, 7n, 15, 39, 43-44, 60, 67-68, 70n.
Allegory of the Cave, 12, 55.
celestial body, 44n.
chance, 21, 66n, 76-77.
chance homonymy, 16, 71n.
Charles-Saget, Annick, intro i, 44n, 82.
choregos, 33.
Cilento, Vicenzo, 8, 40n, 82.
coherence in Plotinus, intro ii, 51 & n, 73-74.
conferences, 1, 2, 76.
consciousness, 8 & n, 29, 37, 44-45, 68-69, 77.
consistency in Plotinus: see coherence
contemplation, 6, 8-9n, 18, 19, 23-24, 27-28, 76-77.
continuity of Soul with Intellect, 25-26.
Cratylus, intro, i, iii, 3n, 12-13, 13n, 19-20.
Crome, Peter, 11-12n, 83.

D

Deck, John N., 17n, 42n, 83.
derivation, 16, 21-22, 24, 30, 35, 37, 46, 60, 70n.
declaring the One, 59-60n.
definition, 4n, 6, 15, 55, 61n.
dialectic, 1, 4-5, 7-8, 22, 23-24, 26, 28-29, 31, 38n, 45, 50, 54n, 60, 63.
dialogue of the soul, 5 & n, 8, 22, 45.
Dialogues of Plato, 26, 75-76, 78.
dianoia, 5, 9n, 22, 24, 41.
diexodos, 21, 45, 50, 56.
disclosing the One, 59-60n.
discursiveness: see *diexodos*
discussing the One, 59-60n.
disembodied soul, 45.
distinctions, 25, 31n, 39-44, 59.
dividing intellect, 25-26, 37-39, 41.
doxa, 6, 13, 21-22, 23 & n.

104

E

embodied soul, 8n, 9, 24, 25-26, 44-45.
Eon, Alain, 1n, 83.
epibole, 69, 71-72n.
epinoia, 39-41.
eternity, 7, 8-9n, 11, 17, 23, 33, 34, 50-54, 51n, 67.
etymology, intro i, 20-22.
eudaimonia, 76.
explication, 19 & n, 34.

F

falsehood, 15-16, 21, 23, 63-64.
Ferwerda, R., 11-12n, 83.
first principle: see *arche*
flux, 12-13.
freedom, 62, 65-66.
Forms, 5, 12 & n, 13-15, 16, 19n, 23, 26, 28-29, 31 & n, 32, 39, 44, 53, 54n, 56-57, 64, 67, 79.

G

generic being, 38-39n.
genus, 14-15, 30-31, 31nn, 32-36, 38-39, 38-39n, 40, 51-52.
going forth, 52-53, 60, 67, 69-70, 70n.
Good, see The Good
Gnostics, 7n, 40, 42, 66n.
Graeser, Andreas, 55n, 83.

H

Hadot, Pierre, 68n, 83.
Harder, Richard, 8n, 83.
Henry, Paul, 2n, 62, 84.
hexis, 25, 29, 37-38, 38n.
hoion, 62-63, 65 & n, 68-70, 71-72n.
higher and lower levels, 17-20, 25-26, 38-39n, 47.

homonymy, 15-17, 16-17n, 71n.
hypernoesis, 65-71, 71-72n.
hypostasis, 42 & n, 65-66n.
hypothetico-deductive method, 73-74.

I

identity, 13-16, 20, 26, 34-35.
imagination, 5n, 8-9, 9n, 22, 37, 45, 77.
imaging, 15-20, 16-17n, 25-26, 27-28, 37, 41, 55-56, 59-60n, 64-65, 70-71.
imitation, 19-20.
immutability, 51-53.
imperfect act, 52.
impressions, 8n, 22, 28n, 37.
improper speech, 62-67, 72.
indicating, 61-62.
Intellect, 14-24, 25-26, 49-57, 65-72, and *passim*.
intellect in us: see dividing intellect
intelligible, 8-9 & n, 11-12 & n, 14-16, 26-36, 37, 43-44, 53-57, 54n, 56n, 72, 75, 78-79.
intelligible numbers, 54n.
intelligible world, 9, 11, 12 & n, 17, 23-24, 28, 31, 38, 42-45, 56.
intuition: see *noesis*
investigation, 76-77.
isomorphism of thought and language in stoicism, 55.

J

judgment, 6.

K

katonoesis, 68-69, 71-72n.
knower, 26-27, 40-41, 70n, 78.
knowledge: see science
known, 26-27, 40-41, 59, 78.
koine ennoia, 21.

STUDIES IN THE HISTORY OF PHILOSOPHY